D1758562

UNDERWEAR
FASHION IN DETAIL

UNDERWEAR
FASHION IN DETAIL

ELERI LYNN

PHOTOGRAPHS BY RICHARD DAVIS
DRAWINGS BY LEONIE DAVIS

V&A PUBLISHING

Acknowledgements

I would like to thank the following people for their encouragement, expertise, and assistance. Firstly, very special thanks are due to Leonie Davis and Richard Davis for their invaluable and manifold contributions. At the V&A, I would like to thank Claire Wilcox for all her guidance and support. Thanks too to the staff of the Furniture, Textiles & Fashion Department, particularly Susan North, Edwina Ehrman, Sarah Medlam, Sonnet Stanfill, Suzanne Smith, and Christopher Wilk. Thanks to the Textiles Conservation Department, notably Lara Flecker, Sam Gatley, Keira Miller, Frances Hartog and Marion Kite. Thanks to Frances Ambler and Mark Eastment of V&A Publishing, to copy-editor Rachel Malig and designer Lizzie Ballantyne. Thanks also to James Stevenson, Sara Hodges, Stephanie Cripps, Jan Bourne, and Cassie Williams. Outside the V&A, I would like to thank Rootstein for the generous loan of their display mannequins. For sharing their expertise with me, sincere thanks to Miles Lambert at Manchester City Galleries, Rosemary Harden at the Fashion Museum in Bath, the Fashion and Textiles Museum in London, Colleen Gau, Amy de la Haye, Caroline Lockwood at the Symington Collection, Gerald Chevalier at Christian Dior, Honor Godfrey at the Wimbledon Lawn Tennis Museum, and Madeleine Ginsburg. Thanks also to Kelly Owens, Matthew Greer, Bella Ritchie, and Carly Eck. Warmest thanks to my family and friends, and of course, to Luke.

First published by V&A Publishing, 2010
V&A Publishing
Victoria and Albert Museum
South Kensington
London SW7 2RL

© The Board of Trustees of the Victoria and Albert Museum, 2010

The moral right of the author has been asserted.

ISBN 978 1 85177 616 0

Library of Congress Control Number 2010923040

10 9 8 7 6 5 4 3 2 1
2014 2013 2012 2011 2010

Every effort has been made to seek permission to reproduce those images whose copyright does not reside with the V&A, and we are grateful to the individuals and institutions who have assisted in this task. Any omissions are entirely unintentional, and the details should be addressed to V&A Publishing.

Designer: Lizzie Ballantyne
Copy-editor: Rachel Malig

New photography by Richard Davis, V&A Photographic Studio
Drawings by Leonie Davis

Front jacket illustration: Corset. Britain or Germany, c.1890. V&A: T.90&A-1984 (see p.90).
Back jacket illustration, left: Negligee. France, c.1932. V&A: T.308-1984 (see p.58);
right: Dress, Gianni Versace. Italy, 1994. V&A: T.215-2004 (see p.208).
Frontispiece: Underbust corset, Rigby & Peller. Britain, 1996. V&A: T.469-1996 (see p.210).
p.6 Wedding corset, Edwin Izod. Britain, 1887. Given by Miss Benjamin. V&A: T.265-1960.
p.142 Bustier, Kestos. Britain, 1953. Given by the late Ruth Sheradski. V&A: T.294-1977.

Printed in Singapore by CS Graphics

V&A Publishing
Victoria and Albert Museum
South Kensington
London SW7 2RL
www.vandabooks.com

CONTENTS

INTRODUCTION

Without proper foundations there can be no fashion. Christian Dior, 1954[1]

Over the centuries, fashion has imposed repeated changes upon the body. The fashionable figure has been variously slim and voluptuous, flat-chested and buxom, androgynous and matronly, and even distorted, with wasp-waists and exaggerated buttocks. Dramatic adjustments in silhouette often occurred very quickly, and were achieved only with the aid of underwear. It is only since the 1960s that women have been expected to embody the fashionable ideal by way of diet and exercise and without the aid of foundation garments, so understanding underwear is fundamental to our appreciation of fashion history. It is also important for cultural and social historians, to whom it provides a symbol of changing social mores and attitudes to morality, sex, beauty and gender.

The Victoria and Albert Museum holds one of the most important collections of historical and fashionable dress in the world, including rare undergarments from the sixteenth century to the present day. This book is the first to be published about the Museum's underwear collection, and illustrates a range of fascinating and alluring items – from structural corsets and crinolines to diaphanous slips and suspender belts – many of which have never before been photographed or displayed.

For the purpose of this book, underwear is defined as private clothing; that is, apparel not intended for public view. This definition includes all types of garment hidden under external layers of dress, such as lingerie and foundationwear, and some hosiery. It also includes nightwear, and intimate garments worn within the home or bedroom. Both men's and women's underwear is included, though the majority is womenswear, which accurately reflects the emphasis of the collection. In contrast to female underwear – which was designed to shape and decorate the body – men's underwear was primarily designed for comfort and practicality, and compared to women's underwear, few items survive; those that do are generally plain and functional, and have been well worn.

Underwear underpins fashion. It shapes the body and creates a foundation for clothing. Even those rare eras that purported to glorify the natural form relied heavily on foundationwear to achieve their ideals, and so for centuries the body has been secretly reduced, lifted, padded, adorned, revealed, and concealed by underwear. This book will explore those structures and functions.

COVERING UP

There is no easier method by which to detect the real lady from the sham one than by noticing her style of dress. Vulgarity is readily distinguished . . . by the breach of certain rules.

Lady Campbell, 1893[1]

In the centuries before regular bathing and central heating, underwear provided insulation against the cold, protected outer layers from perspiration, and protected the skin from coarse fabrics. Covering the naked body was also a matter of respectability and modesty, and underwear served the purpose of concealing the body.

This section includes women's shifts (known as chemises from the late eighteenth century) and a collection of men's shirts. Shifts and shirts were the first and most fundamental items of underwear from the Middle Ages up until the early twentieth century, serving as the base layer for all other garments. They were simple, loose T-shaped garments, and were traditionally defined as lingerie. Though today we understand lingerie to be sensuous or seductive, it is an historically distinct category of underwear that derived its name from the French word 'linge', meaning linen – the preferred material for shirts and shifts. Historically, lingerie was the only clothing regularly laundered. Modern men's shirts evolved from these undergarments, and in some social situations it is still considered a breach of etiquette to remove one's jacket without permission.

Also included are objects such as vests, underpants, nightwear and petticoats, most of which are plain, as elaborate underwear was difficult to clean and was viewed by some as immodest. Concealing the body was an issue of decency and gentility, as the writer and artist Gwen Raverat (1885–1957)

recalled: 'ankles ought never to be seen at all and, if they were, the lady they belonged to was not quite a nice lady. Legs had no value, except that of impropriety'.[2] Respectable underwear therefore represented moral virtue, as an 1861 medical publication called *Hygiene and Medicine*, emphasized: 'the woman's chemise . . . is the white symbol of her modesty, that one must neither touch nor look at too closely'.[3] Covering the body was also important for warmth and health; during the winter both men and women wore wool and flannel undergarments to ward off chills and consumptions.[4]

The chapter also includes a pair of drawers owned by Queen Victoria. Drawers were the first form of underpants commonly worn by women in Britain. They were introduced at the turn of the nineteenth century, and grew increasingly popular towards the 1840s and 1850s when fashionable but flimsy cage crinolines made leg coverings necessary for modesty's sake. Drawers featured a slit from front to back, as closed trousers were considered unhygienic and would have made going to the toilet quite complicated given the many layers that women wore.[5] They were also voluminous, so that the long skirt of the chemise could be tucked into them. Combinations – chemise and drawers in one – were introduced in the 1870s, for a slimmer silhouette, and in the early twentieth century these garments were all streamlined further, evolving into the underwear we recognize today as slips, camisoles and knickers.

 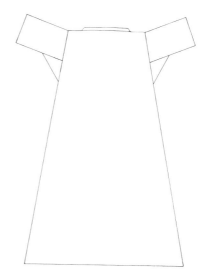

This is a rare surviving example of a seventeenth-century shift. It is finely woven from quality linen, and would have been considered quite luxurious. Fashionable shifts of the time were cut quite low, in order to better reveal the bosom and shoulders.

The shift was the main item of women's underwear from the Middle Ages to the late nineteenth century, and served as the base layer for all other clothing. They were plain T-shaped garments, with gores under the arm and down the sides of the skirt for fit and ease of movement. The preferred material for shifts was fine imported linen, known as 'Holland' after its traditional centre of production. The less wealthy wore linen made from locally grown flax or from hemp.

Shift
Britain, 1673–1718
Linen
V&A: T.467–1997

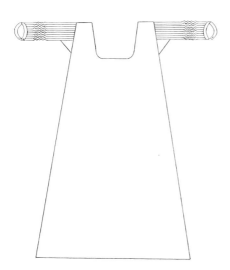 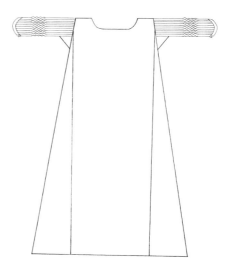

The sleeves of this shift feature fine pleats, carefully ironed into them by the eighteenth-century laundress. Elaborately pressed linen was a mark of wealth, showing that the wearer could afford fine materials and skilled labour. Because households were often large and linen undergarments all looked quite similar, they were embroidered with initials and numbers so that the laundress could identify their owner and distinguish one from the other.

This shift is mid-calf in length and flares from the underarm to the hem with the aid of two long triangular gores. Each sleeve is open a short way up the arm for ease of dressing, and features two whip-stitched eyelets so that it could be tied closed with a ribbon or tape at the cuff.

Shift
Britain, c.1750
Linen, with pressed pleats
V&A: T.25–1969

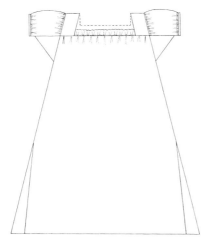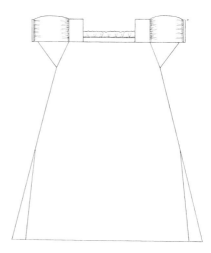

At the beginning of the nineteenth century, women's undergarments were quite streamlined. However, from the 1830s, skirts and sleeves began to grow in circumference and volume, and the chemise became the foundation for an increasing number of undergarments, including swathes of petticoats, corsetry and corset covers. For the rest of the nineteenth century, the body – and indeed the chemise

– would be hidden from view under several layers.

This chemise is typical of the 1830s. It is knee-length and voluminous, with sleeves set in straight with underarm gussets. The linen is very finely and evenly woven, and the sleeves are gathered with minute stitches along the shoulder seam. A cotton frill trims the low, square neckline, which is tightened with a drawstring.

Chemise
Britain, 1835
Linen, trimmed with cotton
Given by Miss Blake
V&A: T.386–1960

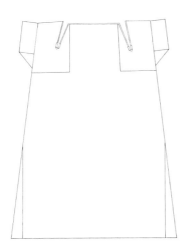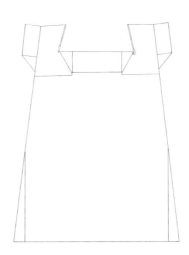

This day chemise is typical of the mid-nineteenth century. It is plain and simply cut, with short sleeves, a square neckline, and an unshaped body. A trapezoidal flap of fabric appears at the neckline, at both the front and back; it was tucked down over the top of the corset to prevent it being accidentally seen beneath the dress. A popular alternative to this integral neckline flap was the corset

cover – a separate bodice worn over the corset (p.24).

This chemise is very voluminous, but by the 1870s the chemise was cut closer to the figure to flatter a new elongated ('cuirass') bodice style. It also became common to see bands of embroidery or open-work broderie anglaise around the bodice and sleeves of the chemise as the century drew to a close.

Chemise
Britain, 1850s
Linen, with run and fell seams and narrow hemstitched edging
Given by Mrs Wyndham
V&A: T.12–1955

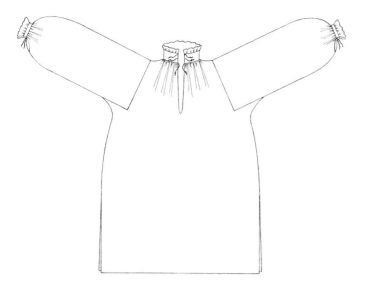

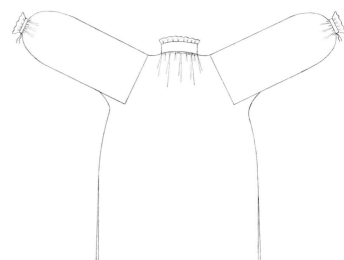

Until the twentieth century a man's shirt was an item of underwear, serving the same purpose as shifts and chemises for women. This shirt is made of 'lawn', a type of linen originally produced in the French city of Laon and woven with a high count of fine yarn for a soft and silky finish. The shirt is typically long, with slits at either side so that it could be tucked between the wearer's legs inside the breeches.

The finest shirts were often embroidered – especially around collars and cuffs. Embroidery was a status symbol, and a sumptuary law of 1533 forbade anyone under the rank of knight from wearing shirts embellished with silk, gold or silver thread, in order to protect its exclusivity.[6] This shirt is embroidered with a foliate pattern in blue silk at the neck, cuffs and seams.

Boy's shirt
Britain, 1540s
Linen; with silk thread in cross and double running stitch, overcast edges,
and seams in knotted and buttonholed insertion stitch
V&A: T.112–1972

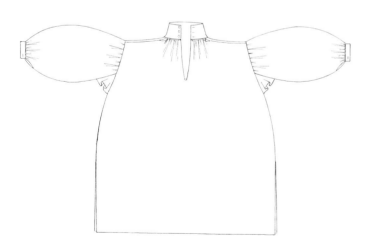

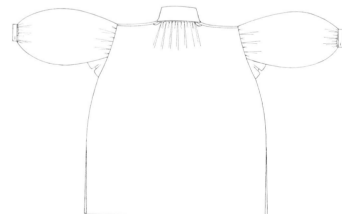

This shirt is made from thick linen, gathered and fastened with circular thread buttons. This shirt was for casual or daywear, and features plain cuffs and a simple high stock at the neck; fashionable dress shirts had ruffles at the cuff and chest.

The stylish eighteenth-century man made frequent visits to his seamstress to talk about 'Linnen and Intrigues', the 'Fashion for Cravats . . . [and] how deep Men wear their Ruffles'.[7] The shirt – as an item of underwear – was often on provocative display, as *The Tatler* of 1710 reports: 'A sincere heart has not made half so many conquests as an open waistcoat.'[8]

Man's shirt
Britain, 1700–1720
Linen
V&A: T.356–1980

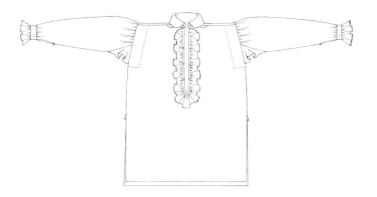
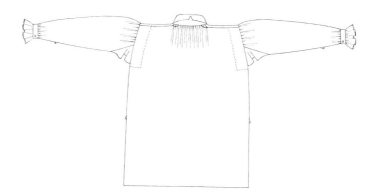

This dress shirt is made of linen, with a high collar and detachable muslin frills at the cuffs and chest. The ruffles at the front are known as a jabot, and flare out over the opening of the fastened waistcoat. The collar was worn up and tied around with a neck-tie.

A well-dressed gentleman wore at least two clean shirts every day, one for day and one for evening wear. A description of the wardrobe of the naval officer, Captain Charles Fremantle, reveals that he owned 56 shirts and 32 neck-cloths.[9] This shirt is embroidered with a coronet to show that it was owned by a member of the nobility.

Man's shirt
Britain, *c*.1830
Linen with muslin frill and Dorset thread buttons
Given by the Earl and Countess of Harrowby
V&A: T.97–1963

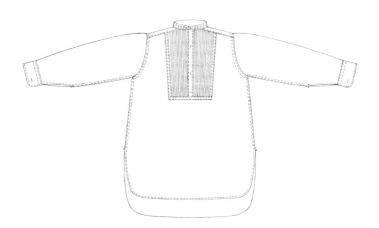
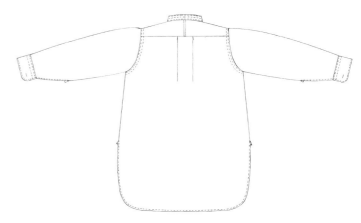

Even into the twentieth century, strict rules of etiquette surrounded shirts because of their traditional status as underwear. In the 1880s, a notice on the tennis courts at Wimbledon read: 'Gentlemen are requested to avoid playing in shirt sleeves, when ladies are present', and shirts were usually covered with a waistcoat, jacket and sometimes a 'dickie' (a starched shirt front). Exposing too much shirt was considered rude, though in the heat of summer a gentleman was allowed to wear a slightly lower-cut waistcoat, as long as he revealed no more than three studs.[10] It was only in the 1920s and 1930s that men started to reveal their shirt sleeves for casual dress.

This shirt was made in India during the time of the British Raj, when the ruling classes observed strict British etiquette even in sweltering heat. The shirt features a starched pin-tucked front, and buttonholes to attach a separate starched collar. In *Man and Superman* (1903), George Bernard Shaw wrote: 'An Englishman thinks he is moral when he is only uncomfortable.'

Man's evening shirt
Asquith & Lord Ltd
India, 1910–30
Linen, with starched and pin-tucked front
Worn by Mr O.L. Rothfield and given by Mrs E.L. Rothfield
V&A: T.241–1962

Asquith & Lord Ltd.

SHIRT SPECIALISTS

BOMBAY

5338

Dressing gowns such as this were worn informally around the home in the nineteenth century, over shirts and trousers, and sometimes with matching waistcoats. Worn instead of jackets, they afforded stylish comfort and warmth without the restriction of formal dress. They were first introduced to Britain around the middle of the seventeenth century, when traders brought back loose but luxurious kimonos from Japan, and banyans from Persia and Asia. They were often T-shaped garments, but in the eighteenth century some were designed to recreate the shape and style of fashionable Western dress.

This dressing gown is made from a warm and practical wool flannel, decorated with applied tufts of black wool designed to emulate expensive ermine fur. It is fitted around the torso and belted at the waist, and features two buttoned straps at the collar and across the chest. It reflects men's fashionable dress with its high upstanding collar and double-breasted frock coat style.

This dressing gown was part of the wardrobe of Thomas Coutts (1735–1822), the founder of Coutts bank, and was donated to the V&A in 1912 by his great-grandson. The donation included hose, flannel drawers, breeches, nightclothes, waistcoats and shirts.

Man's dressing gown
Britain, 1815–22
Wool flannel, with applied tufts of wool, bound with silk twill
Given by Mr Francis Coutts
V&A: Circ.718:7–1912

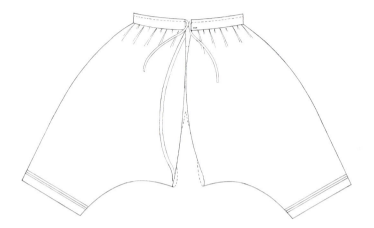

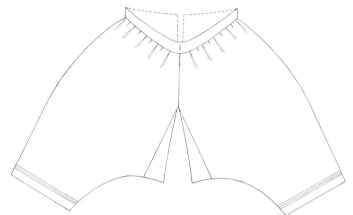

These drawers were owned by Queen Victoria, and are made of very fine, soft linen. They were designed to be voluminous, to accommodate the long chemise that was worn tucked into them, and to blend inconspicuously with the petticoats worn on top.

Drawers, or knickers, were not commonly worn in Britain until the nineteenth century. Early drawers, called pantaloons or pantalettes (long trouser-like undergarments for women), were introduced around the beginning of the century, but were not popular as they were considered too masculine and unhygienic. They were also considered immodest because they were cut quite long and were visible below the hem of the dress.[11]

However, the idea evolved and became more popular towards the middle of the century, when they were cut to a mid-calf length so as not to show beneath the skirt. From around 1830, they were made as two separate legs connected only by a waistband tape or ribbon. These drawers demonstrate this split-gusset style, though they are stitched together a little at the back, showing the move towards closed drawers (p.28).

By the 1840s, drawers were being made in a wide range of fabrics, as evidenced in *The Handbook of the Toilet*, written in 1841: 'It is considered indelicate to allude in any way to the limbs of ladies yet I am obliged to . . . The drawers of ladies may be made of flannel, angola, calico or even cotton stocking-web; they should reach down the leg as far as it is possible to make them without their being

seen.' By the 1850s drawers were positively requisite – the advent of the flimsy cage crinoline (pp.170-74) prompting their mainstream adoption for the sake of modesty and warmth.

These drawers are discreetly embroidered with a crown, the initials 'VR' (Victoria Regina) and the number 6. It was customary to mark household linen with initials and numbers, so that it could be identified and sorted after laundering.

Drawers
Britain, *c.*1860
Linen
V&A: T.9–1968

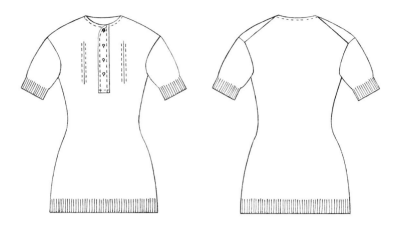

This woman's undervest was on show at the Great Exhibition of 1851, held in London under the auspices of Prince Albert. It is an example of the many woollen undergarments on display to showcase new machine-knitting technologies that allowed for finer gauge knits and better figure-shaping. Wool was a particularly important category in the Great Exhibition, as the official catalogue explains: 'Woollen manufacture . . . has for a long period been regarded as one of the most important branches of our national industry, and . . . furnishes the means of support to many thousands of our countrymen.'[12]

Woollen undervests were worn for warmth and were popular with both men and women from the 1840s onwards. This vest was worn over the corset but, being fitted, was able to maintain a streamlined shape.

Vest
Britain, 1851
Machine-knitted wool with cotton placket and mother-of-pearl buttons
V&A: T.55–1959

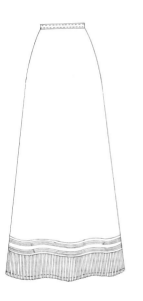

This petticoat is made from plain white cotton, stitched to a cotton twill waistband. It is made to fit the body closely at the front, but is gathered at the back for fullness and a slight train. It would have been worn with a bustle. The hem is reinforced with a thick machine-tucked band and two rows of horizontal cording, under which is stitched a further pleated flounce.

For most of the nineteenth century, women wore several layers of petticoats – the exception being the 1850s and 1860s when the cage crinoline was dominant (pp.170-74). As well as ensuring warmth, petticoats distended the skirt into the fashionable full shape. The outermost petticoat, which might inadvertently be seen, was often decorated with lace or embroidery, but the layers underneath were made from plain flannel or cotton. Cording (rows of twisted plant or textile fibre) was a common method of supporting the shape and weight of the skirts, and as many as sixteen rows of cording and piping can be found on some petticoats.

Petticoat
Britain, 1870–75
Cotton with twill waistband, machine cording
V&A: T.146–1986

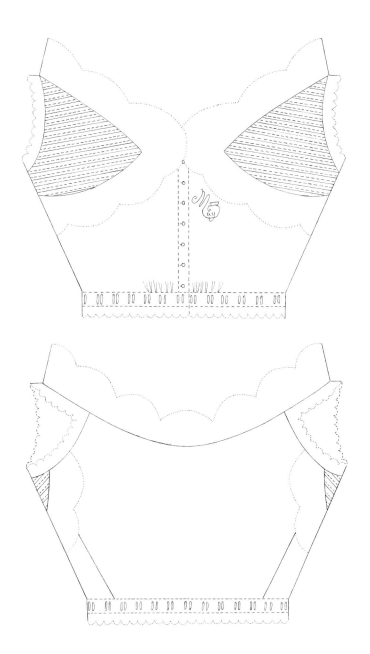

Corset covers appeared around 1840. By 1860 they were commonly worn, along with a profusion of other layers, including the chemise, corset, stockings and garters, drawers, petticoats, crinolines and bustles. Corset covers were light bodices, shaped to the waist, and were worn under the dress but over the corset. They were also known as petticoat bodices, and by the end of the century, as camisoles. They were made from linen or batiste for daywear, from silks and satins for eveningwear, and from merino wool or flannel for winter.

The corset cover provided a layer that helped to soften the edges of the corset underneath the dress. It also hid the top of the corset from accidental view when wearing a low-cut dress. Previously, some chemises had featured a flap of cloth at the neckline that was folded over the top of the corset for the same purpose (p.12).

This corset cover is of fine lawn linen with a crochet lace trim and pin-tucked bust. It fastens at the front with mother-of-pearl buttons. It was hand-made by Princess Mary, who later became queen consort to George V. Embroidered on the left breast is an intricate coronet with the scrolling name 'May', which was Princess Mary's family nickname. Pictures of her around the time she made this corset cover show her to be a fashionable young woman, dressed in glamorous gowns with extravagant trains and bustles, and a pronounced corseted waist.

Corset cover
Princess Mary of Teck, later Queen Mary (1867–1953)
Britain, c.1885–95
Linen with crochet work and pin-tucks
Given by Mrs D.M. Curtis
V&A: T.179–1973

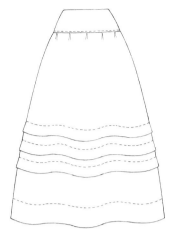
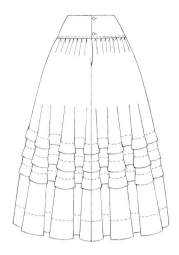

From the 1830s until the end of the century, flannel undergarments were promoted by medical authorities as healthy and warm. *The Handbook of the Toilet* of 1841 advised that 'Ladies should not be sparing of flannel petticoats, and drawers are of incalculable advantage to women, preventing many of the disorders and indispositions to which British females are subject.'[13] Scarlet flannel was very popular, as it was believed that it was particularly efficient at warding off chills, rheumatism and influenza.

This petticoat is mid-calf length, with three tucked pleats at knee level to help kick the skirt out into the desired shape. The flannel is gathered onto a wide canvas waistband that fastens at the back with two cloth buttons. The skirt is fuller at the back, with many more gathers at the waistband. Along with other lighter petticoats and pads, this contributed to the creation of the fashionable bustle shape.

Petticoat
Britain, *c.*1890
Flannel and canvas
Bequeathed by Miss E.J. Bowden
V&A: T.231–1968

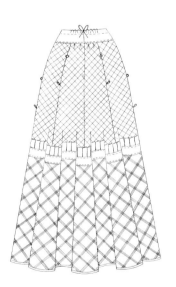

This full-length petticoat features a profusion of flounces, tapes, buttons and loops, and two types of lozenge quilting. The front fits closely to the legs, falling straight down from the waist. At each side are seven pleated flounces that help to provide a rounded, curving hip. The mass of fabric at the back is gathered by a drawstring along the top to fall in a cascade of fabric from the small of the back to the train. At each buttock and hip is a button, and below that a loop, that allows the petticoat to be gathered up and buttoned into a bustle as required. It would have been worn over a small bustle pad (pp.176-8), which was itself worn over a cotton or linen petticoat and a chemise or combinations (p.28). Inside are tapes that tie together to adjust the petticoat's shape and hold it in position.

Petticoat
Britain, 1885–1900
Quilted silk satin, lined with cotton
Given by Mrs George Wade
V&A: T.60–1927

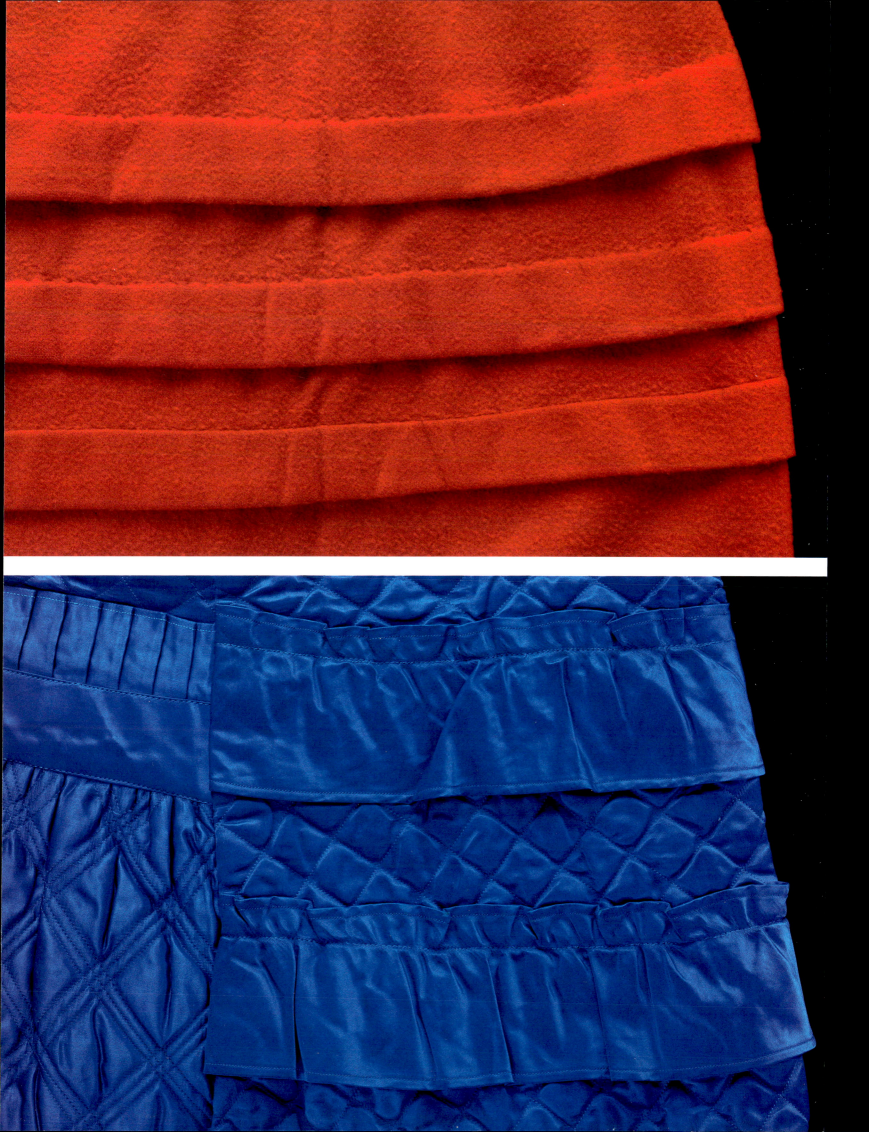

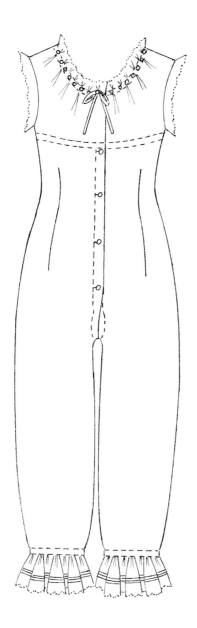
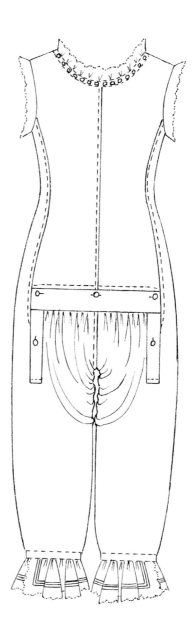

Towards the end of the 1860s the bell-shaped crinoline was giving way to a slimmer silhouette, and in the mid-1870s 'combinations' were introduced. Essentially drawers and chemise combined, they helped to reduce the bulk underneath the new figure-hugging fashions, and were worn underneath the corset, as the base layer for all other items of clothing. They became increasingly popular and were worn into the 1910s; *The Lady's Realm* of 1903 stated that two dozen combinations would not be too many, recommending twelve of thick silk and wool mix for winter and twelve of fine silk or gauze for summer.[14]

These combinations are made of cotton with whitework insertions and Bedfordshire Maltese lace – a lace hand-made with a thick thread for speedy production which nonetheless had a short heyday due to the commercial expediency of machine lace. They are threaded through with green baby-ribbon. The combinations are cut close to the body with tucks to gather them at the waist, and fasten at the front with cotton washing buttons. They are gathered at the knee with a frill of lace, and feature a buttoned flap at the bottom which was known colloquially as the 'access hatch' or 'drop seat'.

The label shows it was sold at Robinson & Cleaver London, a luxury department store specializing in Irish linen goods.[15]

Combinations
Robinson & Cleaver
Northern Ireland, *c*.1895
Cotton trimmed with Bedfordshire Maltese lace and silk baby-ribbon
Given by Mrs Raper
V&A: T.15–1958

Until the eighteenth century, separate nightclothes were only worn by the very wealthy, and most women wore the day chemise, or versions of it, to bed. As the nightdress developed its own identity into the nineteenth century, it became longer but remained very plain, and it was not until 1880 that it was regularly decorated with lace, frills and ribbons. In *The Lady's Realm* of April 1901, the fashion writer Mrs Eric Pritchard wrote: 'the most virtuous of us are now allowed to possess pretty undergarments, without being looked upon as suspicious characters'. Edwardian nightdresses still covered the body, but they created a stylized sensuality of elaborate and feminine trimmings.

This nightdress is made of white cotton, with intricately worked bodice and sleeves. The front of the bodice and the small V-shaped yoke at the back are decorated with embroidered insertions and Maltese-type English bobbin lace. Flowers and butterflies are embroidered in white cotton with buttonhole, chain, satin, long, and short stitches, with laid work, cutwork and needlepoint fillings. Two of the butterflies' upper wings are made of detached pieces of needlelace. The bodice is pin-tucked below the yoke, allowing the fabric to blouse over the waist in the pouter-pigeon style fashionable in 1905. Embroidered insertions around the waist are threaded through with ribbon. The sleeves and cuffs are decorated with a strip of Maltese lace between embroidered insertions, and the cuffs are finished with a muslin frill and silk satin ribbon bows.

This nightdress was made by Lilian Rowarth as her examination piece for the Royal School of Needlework.

Nightdress
Lilian Ethel Rowarth (b. 1868)
Britain, 1905
Cotton, muslin and silk ribbon; with embroidery, bobbin and Maltese lace, cutwork and pin-tucks
Given by Dr Kane
V&A: T.3–1960

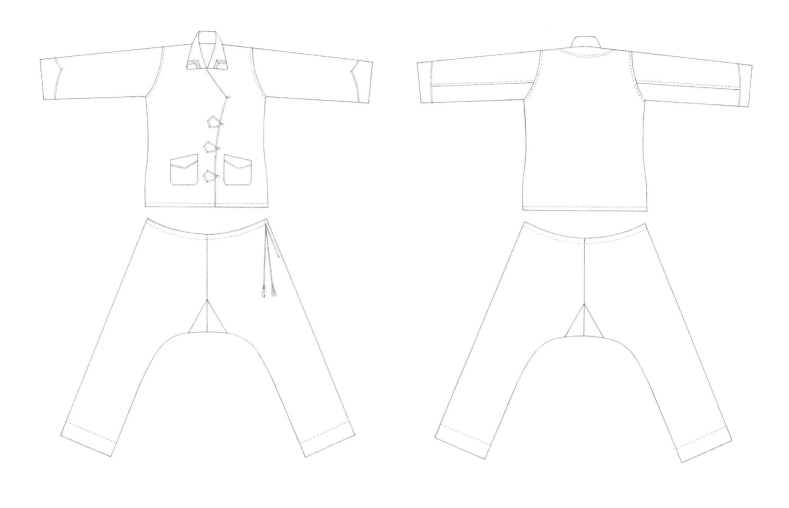

Pyjamas were first mentioned in British fashion magazines around 1880. They are of South Asian origin, where the word 'paijama' referred to loose and lightweight trousers worn by both men and women. During the time of British rule in India, they were exported back to England, and then to Europe and America. Promoted as nightwear for men – an alternative to the nightshirt – they were thought of as something of a novelty and not generally adopted.

Pyjamas gained in popularity at the beginning of the 1910s, when Eastern patterns, tunics and harem pants were fashionable. However, their heyday came after the end of the First World War, when youthful designs and lifestyles came to the fore. They were worn as nightwear by both sexes, but for women they also replaced tea gowns as negligee and informal dress around the home. They echoed the prevailing fashions with boyish, waistless cuts such as this in the 1920s, and slinky bias satins in the 1930s.

They were often exotic, designed with Asian motifs and bright colours, though many were plain or featured traditional lingerie decoration such as lace yokes and frills.

Pyjama suits became increasingly popular as lounge and smoking suits, and were worn with heels and jewellery for entertaining at home. They were the first fashionable form of trousers for women, and in the early 1930s they were also commonly worn as casual beach and holiday wear. By the mid-1930s, fashion magazines were advertising evening pyjama suits for dinner engagements, though only daring women wore trousers for formal occasions. Designers compromised, and as *The Times* of 13 August 1930 reports: 'Pyjamas are made with very wide trousers, which almost give a skirt effect.'

These pyjamas are made of fine silk, with a simple white bias tape detail at the front fastening, pockets, collar and cuff. The trousers are voluminous, but gathered at the waist by a drawstring.

Woman's pyjama suit
Britain, 1920s
Silk, with silk bias tape and drawstring waist
V&A: T.853&A–1974

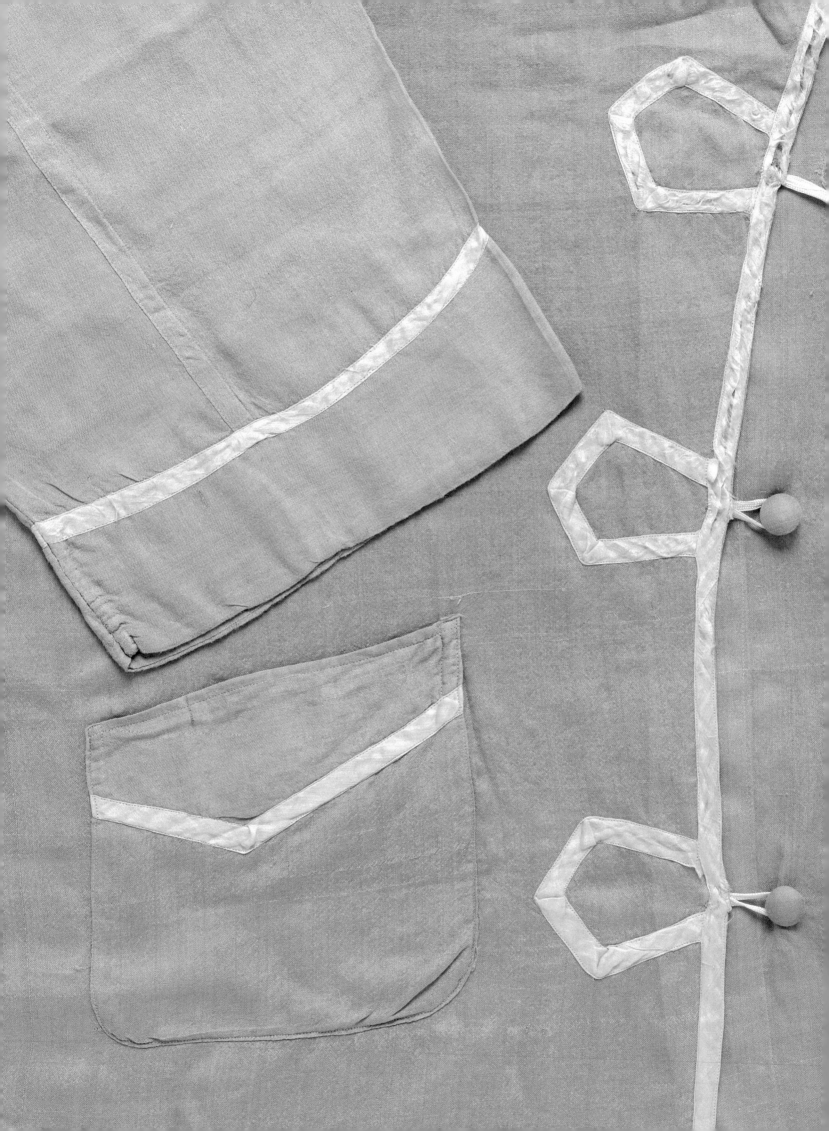

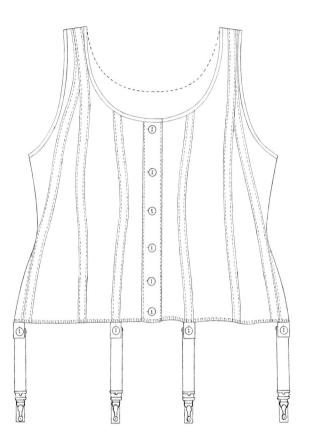
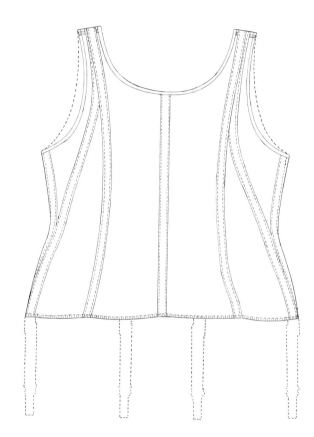

The Symington Corset Company started as a small workshop in 1850. Part of its normal output was the production of stay bands and corsets for children, which were considered necessary to ensure that children grew up with good postures and figures. Babies and young children of both sexes wore vests, called stay bands, which were stiffened with strips of cording. In 1908, Frederick Cox, a director of Symington, introduced the Liberty Bodice for children. Made of knitted cotton, reinforced with strips of cloth, and fastened at the front with bone or rubber buttons, it was advertised as a healthy alternative to stay bands. Symington made over three million Liberty Bodices a year, and most children growing up between 1908 and the 1950s wore one at some point.

In 1912 the Liberty Bodice for women was introduced. It was marketed as a flexible and healthy figure support, particularly for games and sports. During the First World War, Symington advertised it as an essential garment for war work: 'Women who work should not forego all support for their figures. The "Liberty Bodice" gives them entire freedom of movement with the right amount of support. Carries all the weight of the underclothes and pull of suspenders from the shoulders. It also allows free expansion for breathing and promotes an easy grace. Flexible, porous and hygienic. Highly recommended by Doctors and Physical Drill Instructors, for those interested in war-work, sport or gymnastics.'[16]

This Liberty Bodice is made for an adult woman. It features integral suspenders and is fleece-lined – a feature introduced in 1927. One of the primary uses of the Liberty Bodice was warmth, and the advent of central heating in the 1950s resulted in a steady decline of sales. Symington finally stopped production of the Liberty Bodice in 1974.[17]

Liberty Bodice
R. & W.H. Symington & Co. Ltd
Britain (Leicestershire), mid-20th century
Knitted cotton, with tape and rubber buttons
V&A: T.262–1981

Peter Pan
REG.
LIBERTY BODICE
Made in England

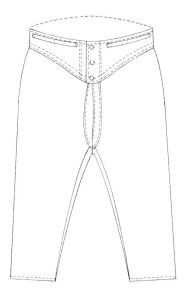
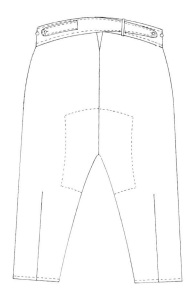

These men's underpants are made of blue silk. The white silk waistband tapers and overlaps at the back to create an adjustable belt strap, with buttons at the side and a gore at the centre back. They are padded at the rear for comfort while horse-riding or cycling.

Underpants were commonly made from wool for winter and silk for summer, and sometimes in bright colours or patterns.

They were worn with undervests, underneath shirts and trousers. Distinctions were drawn between the different kinds of underpants: 'pants' were generally ankle or mid-calf length, while 'drawers' were around knee-level like these, and 'trunks' were shorter still. Throughout the 1890s it was also popular to wear combinations, an all-in-one suit that combined pants and vest.

Underpants
Britain, 1890s
Silk and cotton, with mother-of-pearl buttons
Given by J. Nevinson
V&A: T.345–1980

These jockey briefs – known colloquially as Y-Fronts – were made in the 1980s, but their design remains largely unchanged since their introduction in the 1930s.

Jockey briefs were invented by Arthur Kneibler, an underwear designer for the American firm, Coopers. They first went on sale at the Chicago department store of Marshall & Field in January 1935, and were an instant hit. They were stocked in Britain by Simpsons of Piccadilly from 1938, where they sold at the rate of 3,000 a week.[18]

At the time they were invented, male underwear was dominated by long johns, with only a little competition from boxer shorts, neither of which offered any support. The only garment that offered support was the jock-strap, named after bicycle couriers, or 'jockeys', as they were known. Kneibler adapted the jock-strap to create jockey briefs. Coopers is now known as Jockey International, and for many years was the largest and most successful manufacturer of men's underwear.

Jockey briefs
Jockey International
Britain (under license from the USA), 1986–7
Cotton
V&A: T.44–1987

DECORATION

Lingerie must always be very refined . . . Our mothers used to spend a lot of time and money on lingerie and I think they were right.
Real elegance is everywhere, especially in things that don't show . . .
Lovely lingerie is the basis of good dressing.

Christian Dior, 1954[1]

The following section concentrates upon underwear's embellishments. It is largely comprised of slips and negligees, and focuses on the two primary purposes of decorative underwear: the demonstration of wealth, and seduction. Among the objects illustrated are those trimmed with feathers, embroidery, lace and ribbons.

The earliest garment included here is an embroidered linen smock (the sixteenth-century term for a shift) from 1575–85, of the type seen in portraits of Elizabeth I, and is an example of decoration used to demonstrate status and wealth. Fine linen in itself signified affluence, but visibly clean or decorated linen further emphasized the fact that the wearer undertook no manual labour and could afford both the costly materials and their upkeep.

Embroidered smocks were exceptionally luxurious and the practical constraints of laundering undergarments ensured that most remained quite plain. It was very hard to dye linen with natural pigments, and delicate lace and embroidery was easily damaged. Indeed, lace collars and cuffs were detachable, and were always unpicked from shirts and shifts prior to washing.

It was only with the advent of synthetic dyes and machine-made lace towards the end of the nineteenth century that it became possible to create more economical and practical embellishments. Couturiers took full advantage of the ensuing and discernible shift in materials and techniques, with the influential London couturiere Lucile

– famous for her sensuous designs – recalling: 'I hated the thought of my creations being worn over the ugly nun's veiling or linen-cum-Swiss embroidery, which was all the really virtuous women of those days permitted herself . . . So I started making underclothes as delicate as cobwebs and as beautifully tinted as flowers . . . Slowly one by one [the women of London] slunk into the shop in a rather shamefaced way and departed carrying an inconspicuous parcel . . . the majority came back to order more.'[2] Another important influence on fashionable Edwardians was the fashion writer Mrs Eric Pritchard, who proclaimed – in her column for *The Lady's Realm* and in her book, *The Cult of Chiffon* – that even the virtuous woman should now wear pretty underwear, and in fact was morally bound to do so to remain attractive to her husband and save him from the sin of adultery.[3]

The lingerie of the early twentieth century was considered an important investment, and a vital part of any bride's trousseau. The mid-twentieth century, however, saw a change in the market. The introduction of synthetic fibres like nylon made elaborate and apparently luxurious undergarments easy to mass-produce and affordable to buy, allowing for greater diversification and experimentation. Today, elaborate underwear is available in a plethora of fabrics, colours and decorative finishes, both as inexpensive high-street purchases or as exclusive indulgences from high-end boutiques.

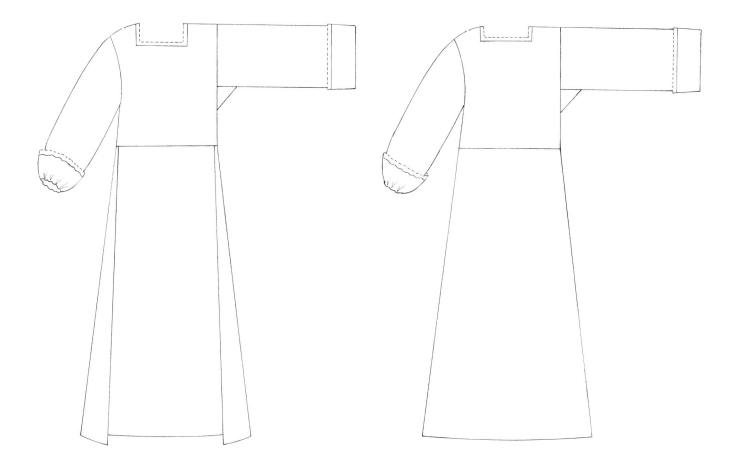

The linen smock was worn next to the skin to protect outer layers from perspiration, and to protect the skin from chafing fabrics. Certain parts of the smock were visible, such as the collar and cuffs, and in wealthy families the smock was often decorated. This smock is richly embroidered with black silk – a technique known as 'blackwork', which was very fashionable in the sixteenth century. It is likely that the black silk was from the Levant or Spain, as it has survived much better than English-sourced black silk whose dye was often so iron-rich that it has tended to rot and disintegrate.[4]

To own an embroidered smock was a symbol of great luxury as it required much gentler handling than a plain linen one. Often, embroidered partlets were worn over simpler linen smocks to give the impression of wearing a decorated smock – a partlet being a short jacket tucked into the bodice, covering the upper chest and sleeves. It is very difficult to tell the difference between a partlet and a high-necked smock in portraits, however the 1575–6 'Phoenix' portrait of Elizabeth I by Nicholas Hilliard shows her wearing both a blackwork partlet and a blackwork smock, in a conspicuous statement of wealth and majesty.[5]

Smock
Britain, 1575–85
Linen, embroidered with silk in stem, back and darning stitches with buttonhole filling
V&A: T.113-118–1997

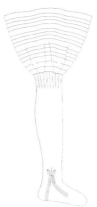

These hose have large cuffs at the top decorated with horizontal stripes, which were meant to be visible over the tops of the oversized boots fashionable during the reign of Charles I (1600–49). They were knitted in the round, in a stocking stitch of fine two-ply wool and embroidered in navy wool with an imitation seam in purl stitch at the back of the leg. They have a band of vertical ribbing just below the cuffs that helped them stay up, though they were also tied with a garter to secure them.

Men's boothose
Britain, 1640s
Knitted wool
V&A: T.63&A–1910

These woven linen hose are cut on the bias, allowing them to stretch and fit to the leg. Hose such as these were often worn underneath knitted silk stockings to provide a smooth foundation over hairy legs and an extra layer of insulation. They were cut in one piece, with another piece of linen for the sole cut on the straight. They are embroidered with pale green silk in detached chain stitch, and also feature lacing at the ankle to tie them tighter.

Men's cut hose
Britain, 1660s
Linen with embroidered silk
V&A: T.126&A–1938

While many stockings were still hand-knitted even into the eighteenth century, the stockings shown here were knitted on a frame. *The London Tradesman* in 1747 reported that: 'Knit stockings are much more preferable in durableness and strength to those made in the loom [frame], but the time employed in knitting stockings of any fineness raises their price too much for common wear.'[6] These stockings are decorated with contrasting green silk triangular gores that run under the heel from one side of the calf to the other. The intricate patterns at the top of the gores were known as gore clocks, and the rose and crown motif was very popular. The technique by which the pattern was added to the stocking was called 'plating', meaning the pattern was interwoven into the knit. Stockings like this were worn by men and women.

Stocking
Britain, 1750s
Knitted silk
V&A: T.34&A–1969

Until the late eighteenth century, hand-knitting dominated stocking production, for although the stocking frame was used to manufacture some stockings (including the previous example), it was not possible to produce them in any great numbers due to the slowness of yarn supply. In general it took eight yarn spinners to supply one stocking weaver. However, in 1764 the Spinning Jenny was invented, allowing eight spindles to operate from one wheel, which vastly increased output.[7] These stockings were frame-knitted with a lighter colour plated into the fabric at the gore, and then intricately hand-embroidered with silk thread in pastel shades of yellow and pink.

Stocking
Britain, 1800–29
Knitted and embroidered silk
V&A: 666–1898

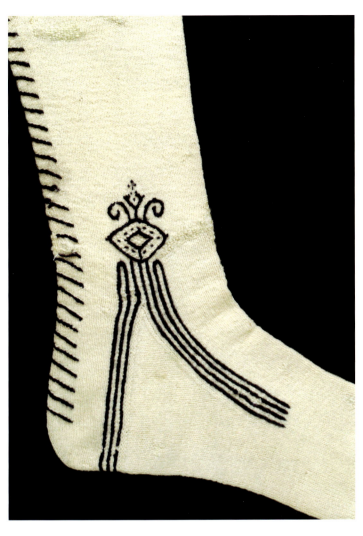

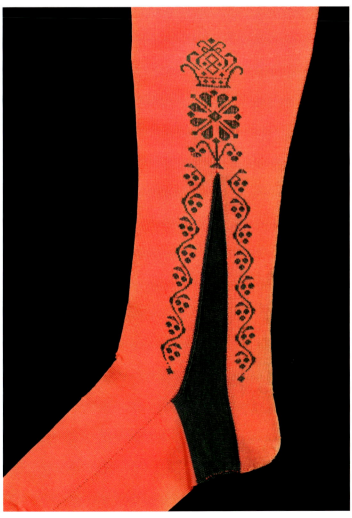
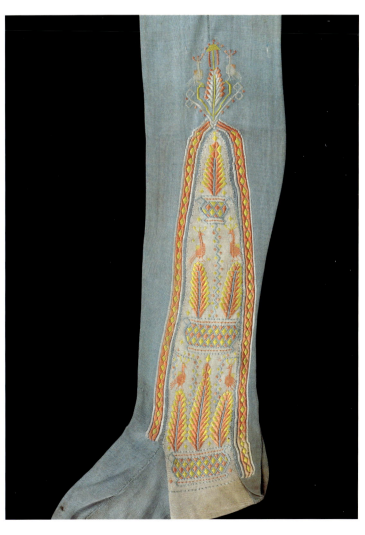

Pure silk stockings such as these were expensive, and even girls from wealthy families were often not allowed a pair until they came of age. This pair was made by the hosiery firm Morley's, who also sold affordable alternatives to silk, with a range of cotton stockings that were chemically treated to resemble silk.[8]

Morley's was established in 1797 by brothers John and Richard Morley, and by the end of the nineteenth century was one of the largest hosiery manufacturers in the country, with ten factories throughout England and a workforce of close to 5,000, excluding casual labour.

Stocking
Britain, 1880s
Knitted silk
V&A: T.47&A–1939

This stocking was exhibited at the *Paris Exposition Universelle* of 1900, a world fair held to celebrate innovations in craft and industry. It is intricately hand-embroidered with tiny beads and sequins, and was shown alongside the other underwear exhibits in the 'Palace of Thread, Fabric and Apparel'. The Paris Exposition was dominated by the art nouveau style, to which these winding snakes belong. The motif became very popular and was used in advertising up until the First World War.

Around the turn of the century stockings were often eccentrically embroidered and patterned, but hidden from general view under long skirts and petticoats as a private decoration. When stockings became more visible in the 1920s they also became plainer.

Stocking
France (Paris), 1900
Knitted silk embroidered with sequins and beads
V&A: T.53–1962

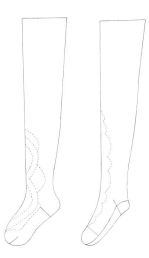

It was only towards the end of the 1860s that a cheap black dye for silk was introduced to the commercial market.[9] Previously it had been expensive and difficult to make, using an iron compound that often caused the fabric to disintegrate. However, by 1900, black was by far the most popular colour for stockings, and nineteen out of

every twenty pairs sold was black. Not only was it very fashionable, it was also practical for the dirty city streets.

It was quite common for black stockings to be decorated with bold inserts, embroidery or patterns. The most expensive of these featured hand-embroidery or hand-made lace, as seen here.

Stocking
Britain, *c.*1900
Knitted silk with silk embroidery
V&A: T.15&A–1956

Stocking
Britain, *c.*1898
Knitted silk with lace insertions and cotton
V&A: T.75&A–1951

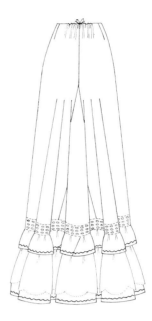

Around 1890 there was an increased commercial availability of silk from the East and advancements in dyestuffs that meant colourful petticoats like this were very fashionable. To be pretty 'is only half of seduction' said one writer: 'Luxury has become the indispensable complement of beauty.'[10]

This petticoat has a deep flounce decorated with machine-embroidered net. The bottom is stiffened at the hem and lined with matching pink cotton to give it shape and help it support the weight of the skirts. The petticoat is slender over the hips and at the front, but a deliberate excess of fabric draws together at the back to create a bustle shape with gathered folds for fullness. The back is slightly longer than the front so that when the vertical drawstrings are pulled and the fabric gathers into folds, the hem of the skirt is even.

Evening petticoat
Britain, *c.*1890
Silk twill with machine net and lace
Given by Mrs B. Oppenheim
V&A: T.6–1957

The early part of the twentieth century saw the introduction of these slim-fitting drawers known as 'directoire' knickers. They were gathered with elastic at the waist and knee and were far less voluminous than earlier drawers (p.20). They were particularly fashionable after the introduction of the slender silhouettes of the late 1900s, which also saw bold block colours teamed with black, as here.

At the turn of the century, drawers – like every other aspect of underwear – became decorative and delicate, trimmed with the lace and baby-ribbon that complemented the Edwardian predilection for indulgent and seductive lingerie.

Drawers
Mrs Fane Ltd
Britain (London), 1910s
Silk satin and elastic
Worn by Miss Heather Firbank
V&A: T.65–1960

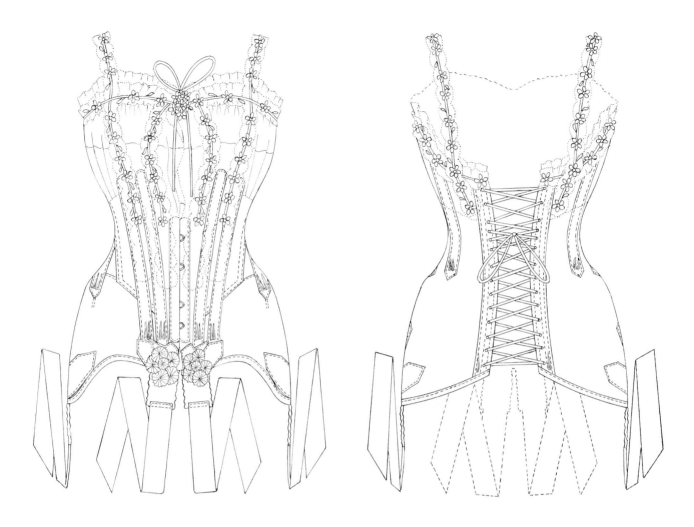

This corset was designed and made for the wedding of Mrs G.E. Dixon in July 1905. When she gave it to the V&A she wrote that it 'was typical of the luxury corset of the period'.[11]

It is an S-bend corset (p.96), typified by the straight busk that compelled the pelvis backwards and the bust forwards into an angled 'S' shape. The corset offered some light control around the lower abdomen with strategically placed whalebones; however – since corsets rely on boning and strong fabrics for rigidity – the insertions here of Mechlin-style lace and fine silk satin between the bones show that its function is largely decorative. The neckline is high, and the entire bust area is made of transparent lace decorated with silk flowers. Attached to the bottom of the corset are four long suspender ribbons, attached with small gathered silk rosettes.

In her regular *Lady's Realm* magazine articles and her influential book *The Cult of Chiffon* (1902), the fashion writer, Mrs Eric Pritchard, argued that attractive lingerie was an important part of the wedding, as a 'pretty compliment' to one's husband. A 1903 article in the *Lady's Realm* advised that 'a touch of illusion . . . with an underlying current of coquetry is permissible in a young and charming bride'.[12]

It was customary for a bride-to-be to buy an expansive trousseau of household linen and lingerie for her new married life, including dozens of nightdresses, petticoats, chemises and combinations, and about four or five corsets. It was usual for the trousseau to cost more than the wedding itself, and was an expense borne by the bride's family.

Bridal corset
Britain, 1905
Silk satin with Mechlin-style lace, chiffon, whalebone and silk flowers
Circumference, bust: 72cm/waist: 55cm/hip: 84cm
Length, front: 47cm, 26cm excluding lace/back: 30cm
Given by Mrs G.E. Dixon
V&A: T.90–1928

London-based Lucile was one of the most important couturieres of the twentieth century. She positioned herself as a pioneer of sensuous, refined creations that were the polar opposite of the heavy flannels of the Victorian age. At the turn of the century she dismissed traditional underwear as unflattering and ugly, and in each of her salons established a special 'Rose Room' selling fine lingerie to 'change all that . . . [making] plans for the day of chiffons and laces, of boudoir caps and transparent nightdresses'.[13]

Lucile's creations were the embodiment of 'the cult of chiffon' promoted by Mrs Eric Pritchard in *The Lady's Realm* magazine, and the Comtesse de Tramar in her book of comportment for young ladies.[14] Both women considered seductive lingerie an important resource and sound investment in retaining the affections of a husband. Mrs Pritchard argued that it was the moral duty of a virtuous wife to prevent her husband from the sin of adultery.[15] She recommended frilly and lacy nightclothes in particular.

Lucile's lingerie – like much of her outerwear – was made from light layers of chiffon and silk, in pale tones trimmed with ribbons, lace and frills. She gave them titles such as 'Incessant Soft Desire' or 'A Frenzied Song of Amorous Things'.

This nightdress does not include a label, but is identical to a design by Lucile, sketched with a lace boudoir cap.[16] It has a low décolletage, lace inserts with satin ribbons, and is made from a diaphanous silk georgette.

Nightdress
Britain, *c.*1913
Georgette and lace, with silk satin bows
V&A: T.1–1973

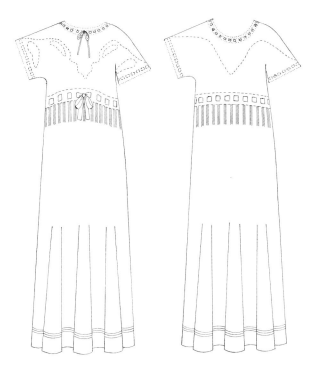

This nightdress is made from white linen, with a triangular yoke of intricate hand-made bobbin lace and embroidery, which extends to the sleeves. The embroidery is inspired by art nouveau patterns. This style of nightdress was advertised frequently in magazines, and was usually shown worn with a boudoir cap.

It was bequeathed by Annie, Viscountess Cowdray (1860–1932).

She was a great patron and often travelled around Europe, collecting works of art. The nightdress has an embroidered coronet on the bodice and is monogrammed A.C for Annie Cowdray. The coronet is a symbol used by peers, though this one is styled in the Austro-Hungarian tradition. She probably acquired this before 1914, after which point England was at war with the Austro-Hungarian Empire.

Nightdress
Vienna or Prague, 1910–14
Linen, satin ribbon and bobbin lace
Bequeathed by Viscountess Cowdray
V&A: T.230–1969

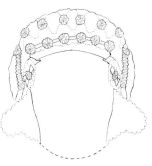

This close-fitting boudoir cap has distinctive wired lappets that curl outwards to form wings. A panel of light blue satin sits at the back of the head, and the crown is of machine-made net. The front and sides are made of open-work embroidered net, and it is trimmed with pink silk satin ribbon arranged into ruches and rosettes.

Boudoir caps varied in style between simple and very decorative ones like this. They were useful in covering unkempt hair in the mornings before dressing. Some women also wore them in bed as a way of preserving their hairstyle, particularly given the time and expense that went into creating some fashionable styles.

Boudoir cap
Britain, c.1924
Silk satin, net and wire
Given by Mr Mather
V&A: T.407–1971

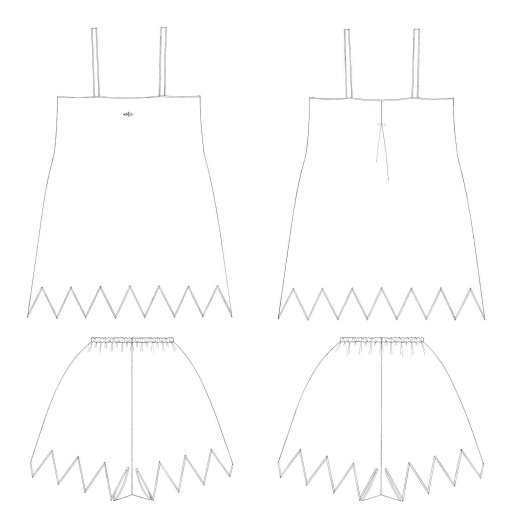

During the 1910s, frilly Edwardian petticoats gave way to simpler layers that streamlined and elongated the silhouette. The type of camisole slip shown here evolved from an amalgam of the traditional chemise and camisole bodice, whilst drawers became wide culotte-style knickers. The result was a sleek line from bust to knee that helped to create the waistless silhouette fashionable with the active, young post-war woman.

The camisole shown here falls straight, with a slight flare at the bottom, and features simple ribbon straps typical of the 1920s. The knickers are pleated and the colours are bold, but the silhouette is simple and there is no lace or appliqué to clutter the effect. For the same ends, suspenders were often abandoned during the 1920s as their clasps were too bulky, and so garters made a brief comeback – especially among the young 'flapper' girls who sometimes wore decoratively hemmed knickers and bright garters with the intention of having them seen as they danced.

This camisole and knickers set was part of Emilie Grigsby's extensive wardrobe, purchased by the V&A after her death in 1964. Emilie was a renowned society hostess who used her vast inherited wealth to indulge in luxurious lingerie.[17] The pieces purchased by

the Museum, which span the first three decades of the twentieth century, are hand-made of the finest materials and trimmings. The undergarments are all personalized with an embroidered 'E' or 'Emilie'. Her taste was for rather bright, bold and eccentric colours and patterns.

Camisole and knickers
France, 1927
Silk
V&A:T.183&A–1967

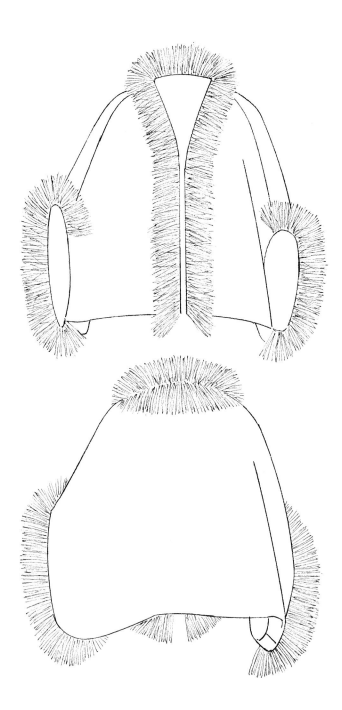

Around the end of the 1920s and the early 1930s, nightwear and lingerie was simple in cut and style, but often trimmed with elaborate lace, fur or feathers. This short negligee is cut in one, from a double layer of a silk satin charmeuse – a weave with a lustrous and clingy finish. The cuffs are the same depth as the garment itself, and the back of the cuffs and the collar are trimmed with white and pink dyed ostrich feathers.

Ostrich feathers were expensive and luxurious but also hinted at the risqué and the glamorous. They featured in burlesque and variety shows, and also Hollywood films; notably – and notoriously – in Sally Rand's 'fan dance' performed at the American *Century of Progress* exhibition in 1933, and as worn by Jean Harlow in the movie *Dinner at Eight* in the same year.[18]

This negligee is made by Rosa Pichon, a luxury lingerie boutique with branches in Cannes and on the Avenue Victor-Emmanuel in Paris. The boutique was particularly prominent between the mid-1920s and the mid-1930s, providing lingerie, nightwear and house-coats, and was listed in magazines such as *L'Officiel* alongside a short-list of high-end or haute couture lingerie providers such as Lanvin, Patou and Rouff.[19]

Negligee
Rosa Pichon
France (Paris), late 1920s or early 1930s
Silk satin and ostrich feathers
V&A: T.262–1967

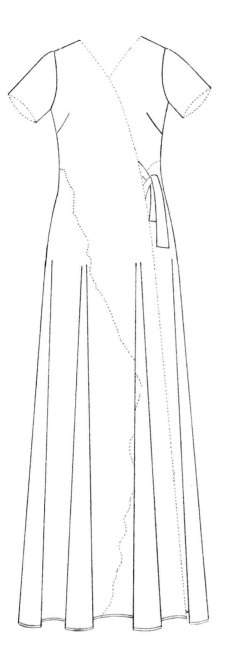
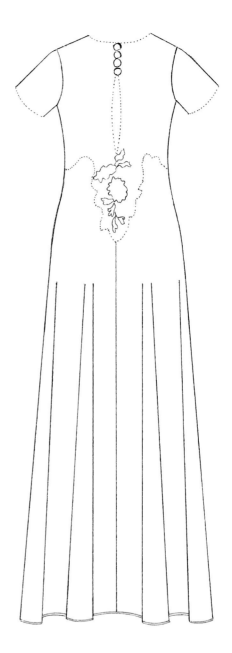

In the 1930s fashion softened and the body was revealed with a clinging definition. Couturiers such as Madeleine Vionnet (1876–1975) designed dresses in fluid satins and crêpes, cut on the bias to hug the figure and skim the body's natural curves (p.196). Lingerie directly reflected this fashion, and both nightdresses and negligees imitated eveningwear with bias-cut satins and low scoop backs. An article in *The Times* of 2 November 1932 said: 'In a season of closely molded figures it is not surprising that the bias line is to be seen in underwear. Nightdresses are cut on the cross . . . backless, with shoulder straps of lace, or with cut-up backs. Trimmings take the form of . . . lace insets or edging,

and embroidery to match the material or the lace.'

This full-length negligee is cut on the bias in silk satin. The top part is made from valenciennes lace, dyed to match the silk. The lace extends from the set-in short sleeves down into a deep 'V' shape at the back, and down the front right side for a wrap-over bodice. The back has a deep slit from nape to lower back, caught at the top with three silk satin buttons. The lace at the lower back is further decorated with roses of appliqué silk satin. The entire garment is hand-made and hand-stitched, but has no label. The colour is fashionably delicate, the favoured colours of the time being coral pink, pale blue and cream.

Negligee
France, *c.*1932
Silk satin and lace
Given by Miss J. Bell
V&A: T.308–1984

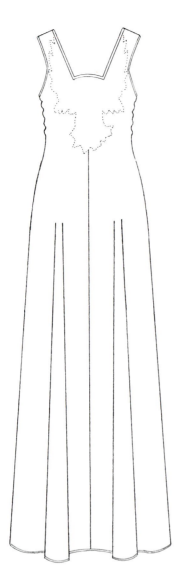
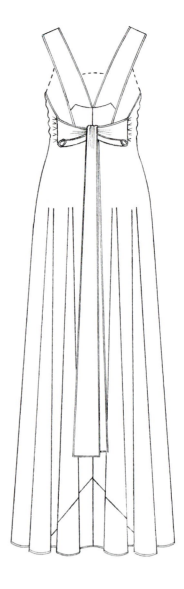

This full-length nightdress of crêpe de chine silk is cut on the bias to cling to the body, imitating the sleek evening dresses of the 1930s.

The bodice is decorated with an inset appliqué motif of a pair of love birds, with their wings extending up towards the shoulders. The back is cut low, corresponding to the revealing fashions of 1930s eveningwear. Two long ties, extending from the front of the nightdress, tie at the back at a slightly higher level than the low cut of the dress, pulling the fabric taut around the waist to further define the figure while revealing windows of skin at the lower back. There are triangular bias gores at the hem to give a flattering kick at the bottom of the skirt.

After the fashion of the day, this nightdress would have been teamed with a negligee, bolero jacket or shoulder cape, usually made of satin trimmed with lace or feathers (p.56).

Nightdress
France, mid-1930s
Crêpe de chine, with appliqué
Given by Miss J. Bell
V&A: T.309–1984

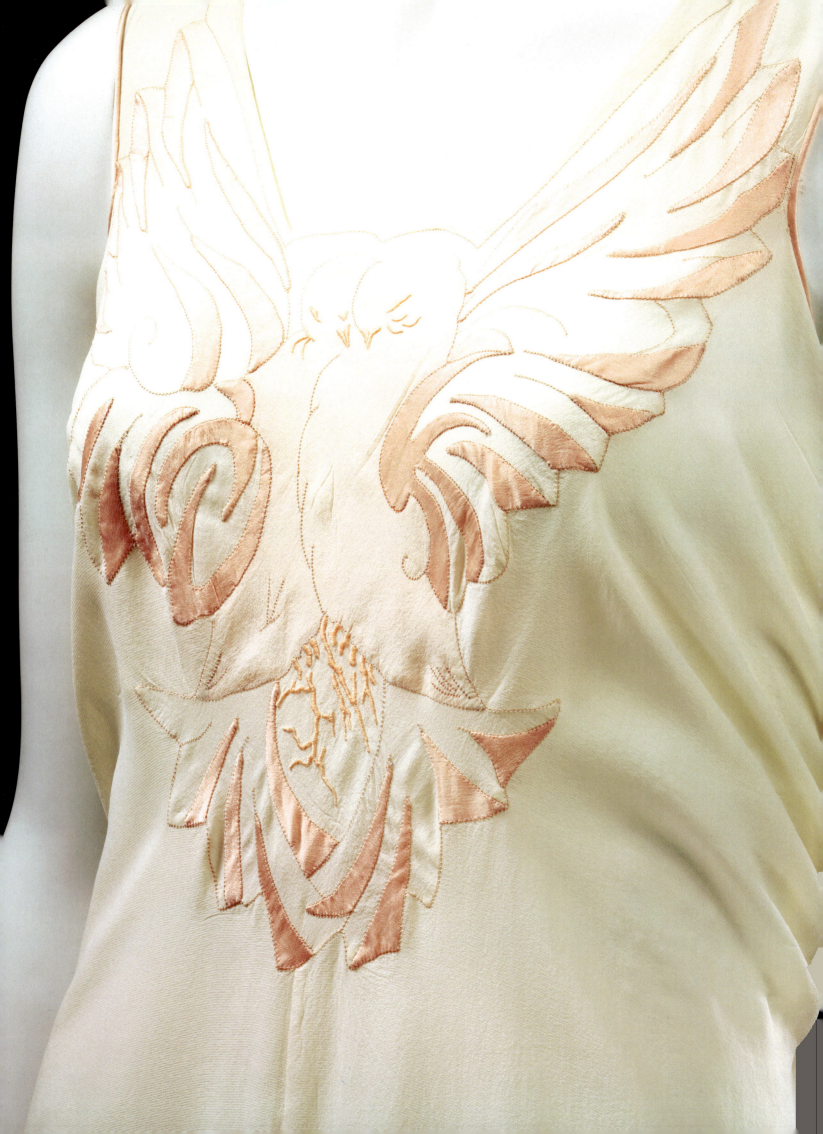

This nightdress is a full-length adaptation of the 'baby doll' night-gown popular in the late 1950s and 1960s, made famous by a voluptuous yet vulnerable Carroll Baker in the 1956 film *Baby Doll*. A baby doll nightdress is a voluminous, usually short, cone-shape garment that hangs from the apex of the shoulders or from just underneath the bust. It reveals the body under the sheer fabric, but only as a suggestive outline.

1950s nightwear was characterized by floaty, sheer fabrics such as voile or chiffon or their new synthetic alternatives. They were usually plain, but may have been trimmed with ribbon, pleats or lace. In *The Art of Being a Well Dressed Wife*, the American fashion designer Anne Fogarty emphasized the importance of romantic and feminine 'boudoir wear' within marriage, saying of nightdresses: 'See that they flatter your figure and that the colours, which are generally paste, go well with your natural skin tone, *without* make-up. Remember – this is one time you can't rely on make-up for your shading. Your boudoir is like the country side. It depends on nature's grooming . . . Have at least six currently new ones in your active sleep wardrobe . . . and think pretty when making your selections.' She also recommended having several tailored robes and house-coats over nightdresses, decorated with feminine ruffles and ribbons, to wear before getting dressed or for intimate dinners at home.[20]

Nightdress
Thea Scott
Britain, late 1950s
Silk chiffon, broderie anglaise trim and silk satin ribbon
T.329–1987

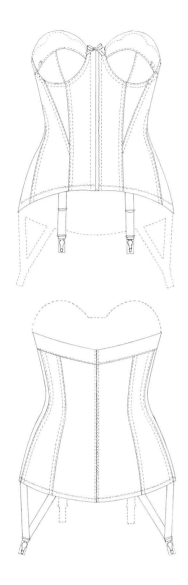

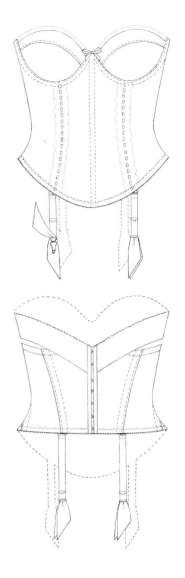

Kayser Bondor was one of the largest lingerie manufacturers in Britain for much of the twentieth century, with several large-scale factories across England and Wales and an output accounting for almost 15 per cent of national hosiery exports in 1949. Beginning life in 1928 as the Full-Fashioned Hosiery Company, it registered the brand name Bondor in 1931 for the French words *bon d'or* – 'good as gold' – and joined with the American firm Julius Kayser & Company in 1936 to sell Kayser hosiery in Britain and Europe. At the end of the 1930s the company was producing over 400,000 items of underwear a week and was the main supplier to Marks & Spencer. The company changed its name to Bondor Ltd in 1946 and acquired the Kayser name from Julius Kayser in 1955 to become Kayser Bondor. The firm was sold to Courtaulds in the 1960s.[21]

This basque is made with bri-nylon, a synthetic fabric patented in 1939 that became increasingly popular throughout the 1950s thanks to its easy laundering and drip-dry properties. It fastens with hooks and eyes at the centre-front, where it is also boned with flat steels for shape. The back panel is made of elasticized nylon net.

Basque (with detachable straps)
Kayser Bondor
Britain, 1950s
Elasticized bri-nylon, lace and steel bones
V&A: T.293–1977

This basque is influenced by 1950s styling, but is constructed using modern fabrics and techniques to improve upon fit and shape. It is made from a satin-sheen Lycra, with an additional band of thick Lycra running from the side of each cup to the top of the hook-and-eye centre-back fastening. This holds the basque securely in position.

Lycra is the now almost universal name for the synthetic spandex fibre branded by DuPont in 1959. It was patented in 1939 and took several decades to develop and perfect, but upon release it was quickly adopted by the underwear industry because its powerful tensile qualities allowed manufacturers to do away with boning and rigid fabrics. It was also easy to wash and dry, and was affordable.

The basque has a facing of pink satin and black machine-made lace along the centre-front and bra cups, which are shaped in the fashionable 1990s push-up style. It also has a plastic centre busk. It is part of an interchangeable set that includes a bra, 1950s-style girdle, and pink satin mules trimmed with marabou feathers.

Basque
Agent Provocateur
Britain (London), 1997
Lycra, synthetic satin and machine lace; with elasticized suspenders
Given by Agent Provocateur
V&A: T.88:4–1997

At the beginning of the twentieth century, petticoats were either styled as skirts or princess petticoats, which consisted of skirt and bodice in one. The slip evolved from the princess petticoat after the First World War, when it was called the princess slip and finally just the slip. It was consistently popular for styles that required a slim-line petticoat to fit beneath the dress, and to smooth over the seams and bumps of foundation garments such as girdles and suspenders. It was popular throughout the 1920s for flapper-style dresses, and again in the 1950s and 1960s when tighter, and increasingly shorter, dresses were in vogue. Slips were made in suitable colours so as not to show, and to camouflage foundation garments if the dress was light. It was only in the 1960s, with the introduction of tights and miniskirts, panty-girdles and jeans, that petticoats and slips fell out of common use.

The Art of Being a Well Dressed Wife, a 1960 fashion advice book, suggested that: 'It is no exaggeration to say that you need a suitable slip for every dress you own, providing the right colour, fullness, and length underneath – at least a dozen half-slips and at least one white whole slip which you will find invaluable with sheer dresses.'[22]

This delicate slip is made from a very light, pin-tucked silk chiffon crêpe cut on the bias, with a deep silk lace flounce and gathered lace bust accented with small pink baby-ribbons. The straps are made of a nude silk ribbon. The development of synthetic fabrics throughout the 1950s allowed delicate lingerie to be commercially available to a mass-market for the first time, largely due to the introduction of nylon, which could imitate costly materials. However, this is a particularly luxurious example of the slips available at the end of the 1950s and early 1960s.

Slip
Britain, *c*.1960
Pin-tucked silk chiffon crêpe, machine lace and ribbon
V&A: T.153–1998

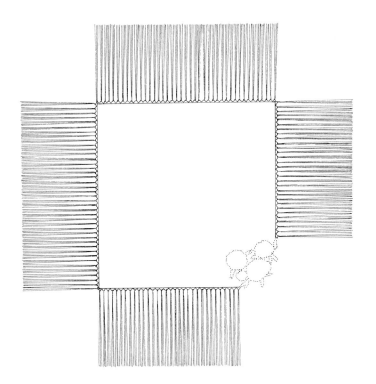

Silky cami-knickers were fashionable in the 1920s, and became popular again in the 1980s, when it was the fashion for women to wear silky and feminine underwear under tailored power-suits and exaggerated shoulder pads. The underwear worn underneath was similarly tailored and sleek, though delicately trimmed with appliqué, lace and ribbon. Underwear often had a deliberately provocative and seductive edge. Basques and bustiers were increasingly worn as outerwear, while stockings and suspenders were once again fashionable, even though tights had made suspenders functionally unnecessary. The idea was that the empowered 1980s *femme fatale* could dominate both business and bedroom.

This garment is entirely hand-made, including the knotting on the fringe of the shawl. The poppies on both the teddy and stole are hand-painted and signed 'Marcel'. Large square scarves were popular outerwear accessories in the mid-1980s, worn wrapped around the shoulders as the finishing touch to cocktail dresses, and so add a glamorous edge to this teddy.

Ian Cooper and Marcel Aucoin were both born in Canada. They moved to London and launched their couture collection in 1979. They used silks of the highest quality and were fond of traditional decorative techniques such as hand-painting and fine pleating. They also developed a technique of using liquid latex and silks that allowed them to apply and seam fabrics together without the use of stitches.

Teddy with stole
Ian & Marcel (Ian Cooper, 1946–92; Marcel Aucoin, 1951–91)
Britain (London), 1987–8
Silk satin with hand-painted silk and fringing
Bequeathed by Ian & Marcel
V&A: T.309:1&2–1992

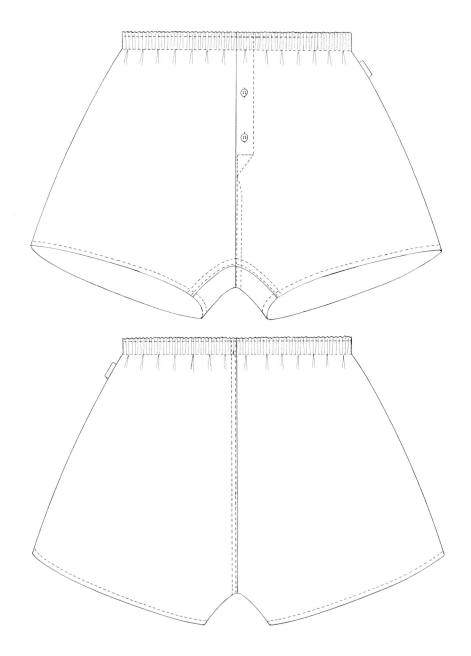

Boxer shorts were introduced in 1925, when the American 'Everlast' boxing company introduced elasticized waistbands to replace the leather belts that previously held up the loose shorts worn by boxers. They were known as 'boxing trunks' and were worn by only a small number of men. They became marginally more popular in Britain during the Second World War, when the Civilian Clothing Act of 1941 – also known as the Utility Scheme – simplified clothing designs to maximize resources and inadvertently improved the standard, choice and fit of underwear available to men. Most British men at that point still wore traditional long knitted underpants or jockey shorts (p.36).[23] Boxer shorts became very fashionable in the mid-1980s, when the model Nick Kamen stripped down to his boxers for a Levi's jeans advertisement and prompted a massive surge in sales.[24]

These boxer shorts were designed by Paul Smith, renowned for designing classic, traditional clothing with a playful and contemporary bent, such as tailored suits in flamboyant coloured silks with vintage print linings. Smith first introduced a line of luxury boxer shorts during the 1980s, when men's underwear started to be designed and marketed as attractive and fashionable, rather than just functional and practical. The shape is traditional but features a bold print of watches contrasted with a bright orange background.

Boxer shorts
Paul Smith (b. 1946)
Britain (London), 1996
Printed cotton
V&A: T.466–1996

CONTROL
AND CONSTRICT

Blind is the man who cannot see
that the form of the corset explains the pattern of social custom.

La Vie Parisienne, 1868[1]

In the late Middle Ages, women wore tightly laced bodices stiffened with paste[2] to control and smooth their figures. In the sixteenth century, however, as the great voyages of discovery across the Atlantic revealed teeming new whale fisheries[3], and rich silks and velvets were imported from Italy and Spain requiring firmer foundations, whalebone became a popular and common material for shaping both body and clothing. Also known as baleen, whalebone is not a bone at all, but the keratinous material found around the upper jaws of baleen whales, used to filter plankton and krill. It is robust but flexible, and can be cut into very narrow strips along the grain. Whalebones were inserted into the lining of outer garments, creating whalebone bodices or 'bodies' that moulded the torso into a rigid and conical V-shape. In the seventeenth century, these whalebone linings became distinct, separate understructures known as 'stays'.[4] The word 'corset' was not used in its modern sense until the early 1800s, during which century corsetry – and the pronounced hourglass figure it created – came to dominate both fashion and social discourse on women's health and morality.

Whalebone was replaced by cheaper flat spiral-steels at the beginning of the twentieth century, and the corset gave way to lighter girdles in the 1920s and 1930s, but in all its forms corsetry was worn by most women from youth to old age and across social classes until the 1960s. It was only then that foundationwear was replaced by diet and exercise as a method of figure control – along with a little help from tensile new fabrics such as Lycra.

The V&A holds a broad range of stays and corsets, which survive in relatively good numbers because of their sturdy construction. The earliest objects featured in this chapter date from the eighteenth century, though the V&A also holds a number of rare seventeenth-century boned bodices and a pair of stays from the 1660s (see 'Fastenings', p.120). A large number of corsets date from the nineteenth century, when corsets were mass-produced. All the objects included in this chapter were designed for women, as although corsets were worn by some men for support and figure-shaping – notably by the dandies and military men of the nineteenth century – the V&A holds no examples.

Measurements are provided for stays, corsets, and girdles throughout the book, for though the idea of the hand-span waist is popularly associated with Victorian corsetry, objects at the V&A and other museums suggest that very tight lacing was uncommon. The majority of the Museum's corsets measure 52–67cm laced closed, and since most women wore their corsets laced fairly wide at the back we should add at least 5cm, and maybe as many as 10cm or so, to those initial measurements. An 1886 booklet on *The Dress Reform Problem* by one E. Ward of Bradford states that 'a distinction should be made between actual and corset measurements, because stays, as ordinarily worn, do not meet at the back ... Many purchase eighteen- and nineteen-inch stays, who must leave them open two, three, and four inches'. To standardize the measurements, however, all are given as if the stays and corsets were laced completely closed. Measurements of length are taken at the centre-front and centre back points, generally following the line of the front busk and the back eyelets. Trim or lace along the top is not included in the measurement.

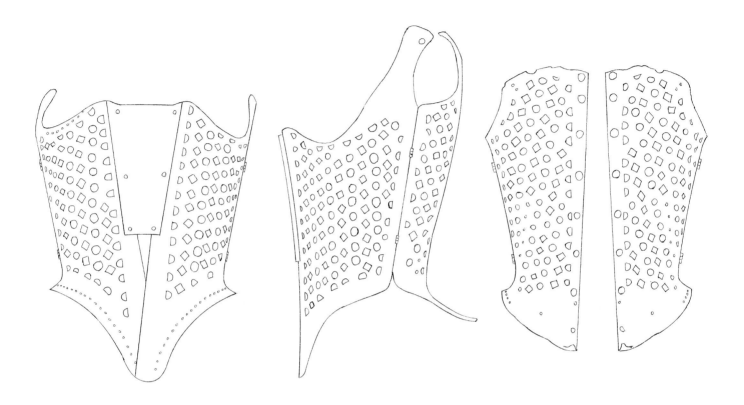

Metal stays are a powerful visual symbol. Yet it is unlikely that they were part of the average fashionable wardrobe; rather, they were orthopaedic devices to correct spinal deformities. Ambroise Paré (about 1510–90), a French army surgeon, described using metal corsets 'to amend the crookednesse of the Bodie'.[5] The majority, he said, were made to manage congenital conditions, although in some cases they were needed because women had habitually laced their stays too tightly and caused themselves lasting physical damage.

These stays are cut low at the front and high at the back. The front tapers to a V shape, and the back terminates in an outwardly curving lip that supports the weight of the skirt and replicates the flared tab shape of whalebone stays. They are made from four plates of iron, perforated with alternating square and round holes to reduce the enormous weight. They would have been lined with fabric and light padding to protect the wearer from chafing edges. They are hinged at the sides.

Because they do not necessarily correspond to fashionable styles, it is difficult to date these stays precisely. Some examples of iron stays in other museum collections are considered to be Victorian replicas.[6]

Metal stays
Perforated and hinged iron
France, 1600s or 1700s
Circumference, bust: 72cm/waist: 56cm
Length, front: 27cm/back: 38cm
V&A: T.231–1914
Given by Mr J.H. Fitzhenry

Until the introduction of the split metal busk in the mid-nineteenth century, a busk was a single strip of solid material that was inserted into a sleeve at the front of stays to keep the torso straight. They were usually made of wood, horn, metal or whalebone, though some expensive examples were made of mother-of-pearl or ivory.

The busk was often given to a woman as a love token from her suitor or lover, with romantic or personal messages carved upon it. The woman, in return, sometimes gave the ribbon that tied the busks in place as a token to her suitor.

The busks pictured here show inscriptions of initials and dates, alongside carvings of hearts and flowers, and reveal varying degrees of workmanship. It is probable that the busk on the left was carved by a professional as a commissioned gift, whereas the other two seem to have been carved in an unskilled (but heartfelt) way.

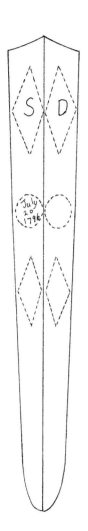
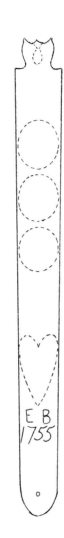

This busk is elaborately decorated with chip carving, including heart and petal patterns. Six glazed inset panels show flowering plants, a rose, crosses, and hearts in paint and gilt metal foil. The painted inscriptions read: 'S.D. July the 20th. 1796'.

Busk
Carved wood, glass, paper,
paint and gilt metal foil
Britain, 1796
Length: 34cm
Given by Robert Holland Martin,
Esq., C.B.
V&A: T.345–1921

This busk is carved and painted with lozenge, diamond, star and heart shapes. The inscription reads: 'E.B. 1755'. There is an inscription on the back, which is now illegible, but looks to be a short poem.

Busk
Carved wood and paint
Britain, 1755
Length: 34.5cm
V&A: T.674–1996

This busk is engraved with two hearts shot through with an arrow, with scrolling leaves and lozenge patterns. Also inscribed is: 'Maria Cooke 1821'.

Busk
Carved whalebone
Britain, 1821
Length: 38.5cm
V&A: 675–1902

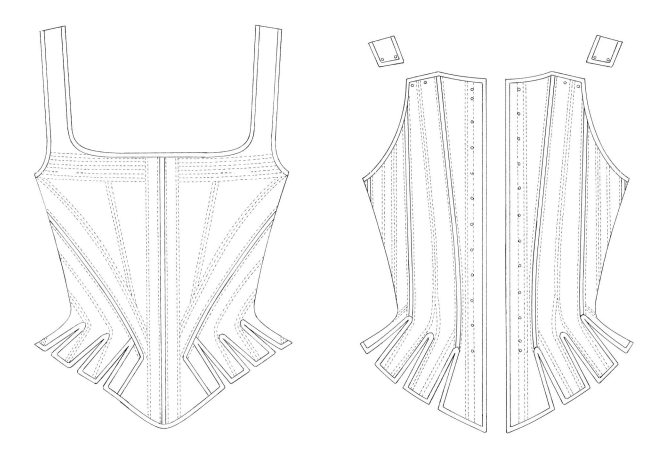

These half-boned stays demonstrate a sophisticated boning technique that uses few, but efficiently placed, whalebones. They show stay-makers' increasing understanding that the direction rather than the number of whalebones was the crucial factor in creating the desired shape, and here the bones are concentrated at seam contours. The stays are made in eight parts, of buckram and silk damask lined with linen, trimmed with a strong twill tape. Pieces of whalebone run horizontally across the bust and are moulded to shape with a hot iron to create a firm and slightly oval shape typical of this decade. The high back ensured a flat and upright posture. They lace at the back with whipped eyelet holes.

From the middle of the eighteenth century, stay-making became an increasingly formalized industry in France and Britain. Scientific and medical systems for measuring the proportions of the body were increasingly applied to pattern-cutting by tailors, dressmakers and stay-makers, who began to introduce measurement sheets.

In his 1769 book, *L'Art du Tailleur*[7], François de Garsault provided a number of patterns for stays, along with detailed directions explaining how the professional stay-maker used them. He began by choosing the appropriate size of pattern from his stock, and then, onto a sufficient length of buckram strengthened with glue or paste, marked out the pattern with chalk. Allowing a thin strip of excess for turning he would then cut out the patterns and tack them onto pieces of calico which were similarly cut and marked with chalk. He then drew equidistant straight lines on the buckram-calico layers with a ruler (roughly about 6mm apart), which when stitched formed casings. By the eighteenth century the stay-maker could buy pre-cut strips of whalebone, which he would insert into the casings before finally tacking the boned pattern pieces together and pressing with a hot iron to curve them into shape. Eyelet holes were then punched and bound, shoulder straps added, and tape stitched round the edges to bind the bones. An optional final stage would be to use the original patterns to create a covering of rich material and a lining of soft cotton or linen.

Half-boned stays
Britain, 1770s
Silk damask, buckram and whalebone, lined with linen
Circumference, bust: 81cm/waist: 62cm
Length, front: 31cm/back: 39cm
Given by Messrs Harrods Ltd.
V&A: T.909–1913

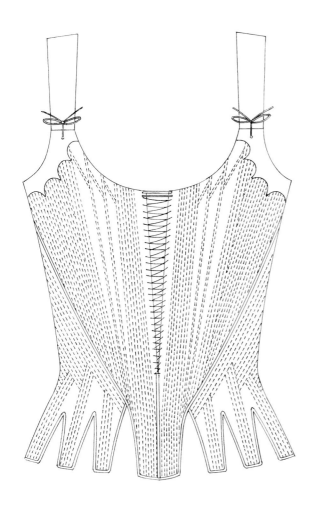

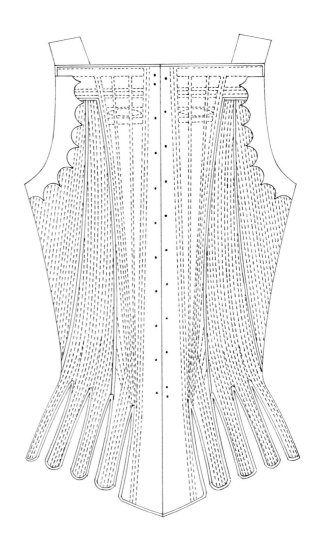

In her 1778 novel *The Sylph*, Georgiana Cavendish, Duchess of Devonshire, wrote: 'Poor Winifred . . . broke two laces in endeavouring to draw my new French stays close . . . Then they are so intolerably wide across the breast that my arms are absolutely sore with them; and sides so pinched! But . . . to be admired, is a sufficient balsam.'

Stays were always worn over a shift, which protected the skin from its coarser materials. However, there is a strip of scallop-edged chamois leather under each arm that shows a barrier was also needed to protect outer layers of clothing from the wear and tear of its hard edges, and to prevent the whalebone ends from poking through.

These stays are made of densely woven linen, high at the back and wide and low across the bust. They are made in eight pieces, with pale blue silk ribbon overlaying the seams. The whalebones are densely packed in fine, hand-stitched directional channels that smooth and press the torso into the fashionable cone shape. The two front panels are seamed together at the bottom of the centre-front tab, but open into a decorative feature of spiral lacing with a single piece of ribbon. The stays fasten at the back.

The bones of these stays are cut very finely, in some instances as narrowly as 3mm. Cutting whalebone this thinly required a high degree of expertise and physical strength, which was also needed to push the bones into their tight fabric casings.

Stays
Britain, 1780s
Linen and buckram, applied silk ribbon, chamois leather and whalebone, lined with linen
Circumference, bust: 86cm/waist: 62cm/hip (over flared tabs): 71cm
Length, front: 28cm/back: 40cm
Given by Mrs Strachan
V&A: T.172–1914

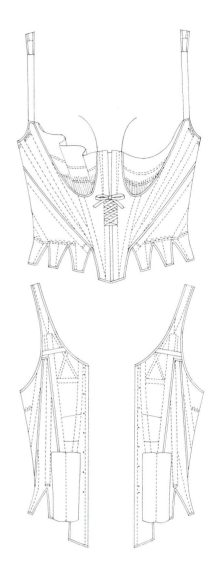

In the 1790s, neoclassical gowns were fashionable. They were made of light fabrics that fell around the body from a high waistline just under the bust. The heavily boned stays of earlier decades (p.80) were designed to create an elongated torso, and were entirely unsuitable for this new style. Stay-makers had to adapt quickly.

These shorter, lightly boned stays were much more suited to the new fashion, with cups that defined and separated the breasts rather than pressing them flat as the old stays did. They are made in eight parts, from cotton lined with linen, and silk tape to cover the joining seams. There are tabs around the bottom, in accordance with the stay-making conventions of the eighteenth century, however they are unboned and sit too high on the diaphragm to serve their traditional purpose of splaying outward over the hips, suggesting that the stay-maker had yet to fully adjust to the new fashion. The stays are very sparsely boned and the cotton so light that cotton twill tapes are sewn onto the surface at the sides and at each shoulder to reinforce the shape and prevent stretching. At the small of the back are two quilted tabs to keep the drapes of the fashionable soft gowns from revealing the arch of the lower back, which was considered indecent. The breast gussets are made of gathered and quilted cotton with small blue French knots around them, and the integral central busk is decorated with silk ribbon. The stays fasten at the back through whip-stitched eyelets.

By the early nineteenth century, stay-makers had developed long corded corsets (p.84), which were far better suited to the classical gowns of the period. However, illustrated here is the transitional phase between the old and new styles, between stays and corsets. Indeed, it was around this time that the term 'corset' (previously used to refer to close-fitting bodices) started to be used as a refined name for stays.[8] *The Times* of 24 June 1795 states that: 'corsettes about six inches long [15.2cm] . . . are now the only defensive paraphernalia of our fashionable belle'.

Stays
Britain, about 1795
Cotton with silk thread, whalebone and silk ribbon, lined with linen
Circumference, bust: 80cm/'waist' (the point just above tabs, corresponding with the lower ribs): 57cm
Length, front: 18cm/back: 27cm
V&A: T.237–1983

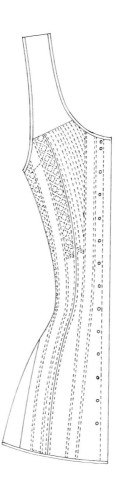
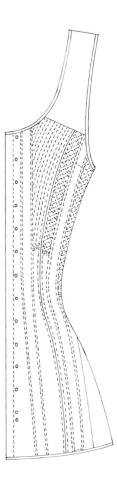

At the turn of the nineteenth century the highly structured boned stays and wide hoops of the preceding decades were abandoned in favour of a neo-classical ideal that revered a youthful, natural body.

The ideal was unachievable for all but girls or the slimmest women, and so corsets were developed to assist. By 1805 corsets were being designed that lifted and defined the breasts, and extended down over the hips to create the fashionable tubular silhouette. During the 1820s the waist moved down slightly from its high position under the breasts, and the skirt and sleeves started to fill out. However, the dress remained closely fitted around the body, particularly at the bodice, and fashionable breasts remained high.

This corset is made from two layers of cotton sateen with a linen interlining. It is made in six panels with two triangular gores inserted at each breast and a larger triangular gore at each hip.

It is very lightly boned at the abdomen, sides and back, albeit with a wide dominant casing for a now absent central busk. The direction and placement of the bones is intended to flatten the stomach but also to radiate out over – and thereby emphasize – the curve of the hips. It is decorated with trapunto work, a decorative but reinforcing quilting technique, which is padded from the underside and surface-stitched to create a raised effect. The trapunto work is concentrated around the diaphragm to support and lift the breasts, aided by the central busk which also divides them. Below the waist the trapunto becomes simple cording, with gores of plain cotton, broken up by the strategically placed bones. The lacing below the waist would have been relatively loosely tied, to emphasize the hips. The armholes are set far back with the straps low on each shoulder to give a wide décolletage.

Corset
Britain, *c.*1820
Cotton with trapunto work, cording and whalebone, with linen interlining
Circumference, bust: 80cm/waist: 52cm/hip: 77cm
Length, front: 37cm/back: 36cm
V&A: T.57–1948

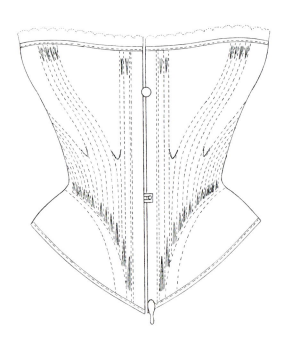
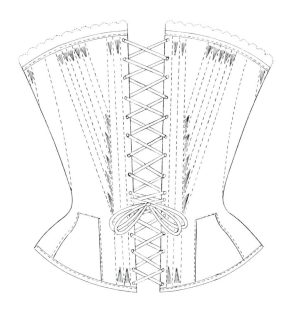

In 1829 the French corsetier Jean-Julien Josselin patented the split busk. It opened at the front and allowed women to fasten and remove their own corsets with ease. Until that point, laces had to be completely removed in order to get in and out of the corset, and assistance was required to tie it properly. This corset features the metal split busk, with metal hook fastenings that still show traces of blue enamel paint. The fastenings are unusual because from the middle of the century most split busks were fastened with the 'slot and stud' system patented by the English inventor Joseph Cooper in 1848 (see page 126).[9]

From the late 1840s to the 1860s skirts were full and bell-shaped, at which point corsets were relatively short and not particularly tightly laced, since the massive skirts made all waists look proportionally small. This corset is heavily boned at the front, but has very little boning at the back, and no boning at all over the hips. The curve of the bones from their low point over the abdomen around to the high waistline over the hips presses into the waist, defining the hipline and the extravagant outward curve of fashionable cage crinoline. Some corsets from this period feature a quilted pad or roll at the bottom of the corset to support the weight and shape of the crinoline. In the 1870s, fashion would demand a more slender, elongated silhouette, whereupon corsets would be boned from top to bottom to smooth and envelop the hips rather than to flare out over them as this does (p.90).

The top of the corset is trimmed with machine lace, and gathered closed with a thin twill ribbon. The bones are hand-finished at top and bottom with flossing, which reinforces the bones while also serving a decorative purpose.

Corset
France or Britain, 1864
Silk, edged with machine lace, with whalebone and metal eyelets, lined with cotton twill
Circumference, bust: 77cm/waist: 56cm/hip: 76cm
Length, front: 33.5cm/back: 34cm
Given by the Burrows family
V&A: T.169–1961

In the latter part of the mid-nineteenth century there was an increase in women's participation in sports, as the moral and physical benefits of exercise were promoted. Women took up a variety of sports, including croquet, hockey, golf and tennis, in addition to their more traditional outdoor activities of riding and walking. Women undertook these activities in full day dress, including their corsets, and the common sight of bloodied corsets in tennis club dressing rooms testified to the pains of the physically active woman.[10]

This corset is one of Brown's 'Dermathistic' corsets. They were widely advertised, ready-to-wear corsets, available from department stores and via mail-order. One advertisement in the *Jubilee Graphic* of 20 June 1887, reads: 'Ladies who indulge in such healthful and exhilarating exercises as Rowing, Riding, Driving, Lawn Tennis &c.

will find the "D" invaluable, the leather being a sure prevention against Bones, Busks and Steels breaking whilst it renders the Corset most delightfully comfortable.' The 'Dermathistic', though advertised for exercise, differs from other corsets only in that the bones are faced with leather to reduce the risk of them tearing through the dress if they should snap under the pressure of physical exertion.

The whalebone casings are stitched directly onto the facing – a technique popular from the 1880s onwards. It features a spoon busk, popular from the mid-1870s to the end of the 1880s, which curves fashionably over the abdomen without – it was thought – pressing on the internal organs. It is trimmed with a deep frill of machine-made lace around the top. Its appearance is striking, but the 'Dermathistic' was relatively affordable.

Brown's 'Dermathistic' Corset
Britain, 1883
Sateen with leather facings trimmed with machine lace, with whalebone, brass eyelets, and steel spoon busk; lined with white sateen
Circumference, bust: 73cm/waist: 56cm/hip: 80cm
Length, front: 34.5cm/back: 39cm
V&A: T.84&A–1980

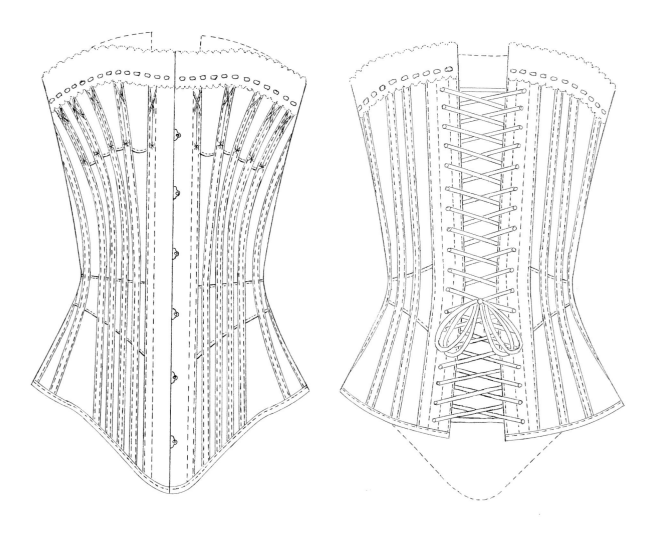

This corset is part of a collection given to the V&A of unsold and archival stock from the Yanovsky corset shop in the East End of London. Mayer Yanovsky ran a highly respected glove-making and corsetry business, which opened in 1887 and was still running until the mid-1970s. Mr Yanovsky made the corsets, while his wife did all the fittings and the rest of the family helped in the shop.[11] Many of the corsets were made on the premises, but before the First World War, ready-to-wear corsets were sometimes bought from Württemberg in Germany, which was a manufacturing centre for wool and cotton.

The corset is made in two parts, bound by a twill weave tape at the top and bottom. The whalebones run in straight single casings of dark brown coutille stitched over the facing of lighter brown coutille. It covers the hips and curves to a low point that completely envelops the abdomen for the tight, elongated bodice of the late 1880s. This corset is shaped with a double busk at the centre-front, boning at either side of the back metal eyelets, and thick side steels. The shape is reinforced with an extra layer of dark brown coutille, which forms a cinching 'belt' around the waist, and a section of corded coutille at the bust with decorative but reinforcing flossing. Each of these features strengthens the corset, minimizing the risk of breakages at stress points, and making the corset fit smoothly and tightly.

The corset has one of the smallest waist measurements in the collection of the V&A, if laced closed to 48cm. During the 1890s, it was fashionable to be voluptuous at the bosom and hips, but small at the waist. Tight corsets aided this by displacing flesh from the waist to these areas.

Corset
Britain or Germany, *c.*1890
Cotton coutille with machine lace, whalebone, metal eyelets, and steel; lined with cotton twill
Circumference, bust: 71cm/waist: 48cm/hip: 71cm
Length, front: 41cm/back: 37.5cm
Given by the family of Mayer Yanovsky
T.90&A–1984

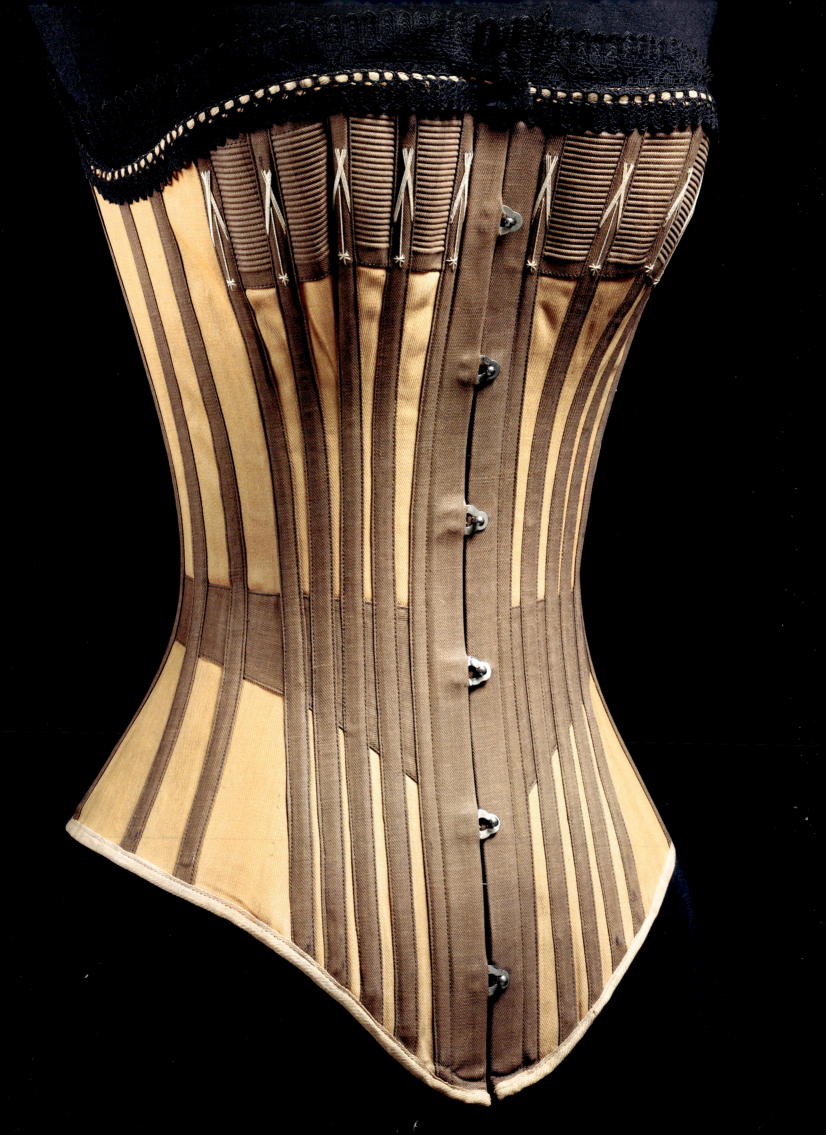

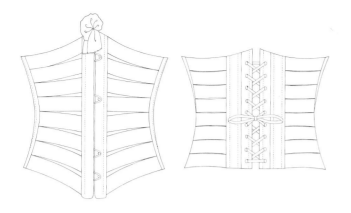

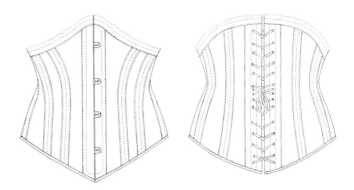

This type of corset was known as a 'ribbon corset', and was favoured by dress reformists for its comparatively minimal use of boning. It is cut under the bust for ease of movement, though it is still heavily boned at the sides and back for posture and waist cinching. The ribbon corset was advertised extensively from 1900 to 1910, and it seems as though it had two distinct markets: as a negligee corset for boudoir wear, and also as a sports corset for golf, tennis or croquet, and even for ice-skating.[12]

Underbust corset
Britain, c.1900
Silk satin ribbon, whalebone, metal eyelets and steel busk
Circumference, waist: 48cm/hip: 50cm
Length, front: 28cm/back: 19cm
Given by Mrs Raper
V&A: T.18–1958

The Aertex Cellular Clothing Company was established in 1888 by Lewis Haslam of Aldermanbury, London. For many years he was a Member of Parliament, but he was particularly interested in health and dress reform, and believed in the health-giving properties of fresh air. He developed the idea of cellular cotton clothing that allowed the skin to breathe. This corset is cut away under the bust and over the hip, to allow relative freedom of movement for sports or outdoor activities.

Underbust corset
The Aertex Cellular Clothing Company
Britain, 1890s
Cellular cotton, whalebone, metal eyelets, and steel busk; broderie anglaise trim (not original)
Waist circumference: 59cm
Length, front: 28cm/back: 27cm
Bequeathed by Miss E.J. Bowden
V&A: T.234–1968

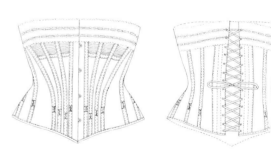

Dr Gustav Jaeger (1832–1917) advocated wearing exclusively woollen undergarments to absorb perspiration, allow 'noxious exhalations' to disperse, and maintain warmth.[13] He was not opposed to corsets, but rather to the materials from which they were made, saying that wool provided a firm figure without the need for tight lacing. It is a typical health corset because it has shoulder straps. Reformists suggested that placing the weight of dress on the shoulders was better for the spine and internal organs than anchoring it around the waist and hips. For more on this corset, see p.130.

Corset bodice
Jaeger Sanitary Woollen System
Britain, c.1900
Undyed wool, ribbed wool cording, mother-of-pearl buttons
Bequeathed by Miss E.J. Bowden
V&A: T.229–1968

This corset is made in two parts, of woven stockinet. Corsets such as this were often worn for the popular pastime of bicycling, as the knit offered flexibility and a bit of stretch. The flat spiral steels are visible in their twill casings, which are sewn onto the surface of the corset. They were a recent invention at the time, and were on show in this way to advertise the modernity of the garment.

Corset
Britain or Germany, 1900s
Cotton stockinet with machine lace, steels in twill casings, metal eyelets; lined with fleeced cotton
Circumference, bust: 82cm/waist: 54cm/hip: 84cm
Length, front: 29cm/back: 26cm
Given by the family of Mayer Yanovsky
V&A: T.93&A–1984

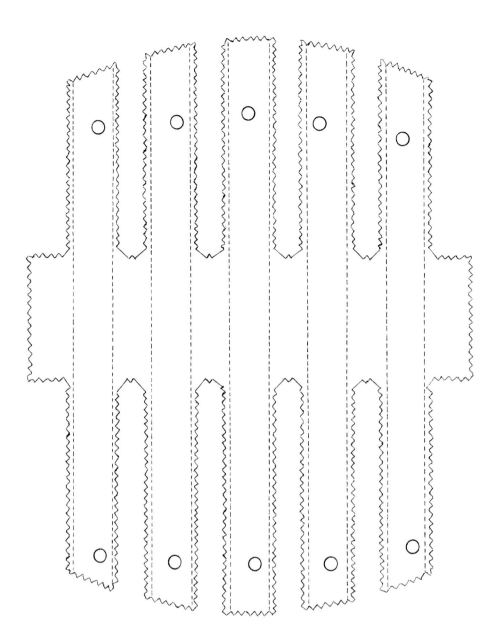

Corsets were often advertised with promises of durability, and sometimes given tough names such as 'Hercules' or 'Armorside'. However, they inevitably suffered from wear and tear, and sometimes broken or twisted bones ripped through clothing or even pierced the skin. Some companies supplied spare bones in the box with their new corsets, and many companies offered repair services. A patent was registered in 1893 for corset shields, which would: 'lessen liability of breakage of the ribs [bones], and protect the body of the wearer from abrasion by the protruding ends of ribs in case of the breakage thereof'.[14]

These corset shields are made of flat steel blades covered in calico. It was around this time that steels began to replace whalebones as boning material, due in large part to the fact that the baleen whale – the source of whalebone – had been hunted to near extinction.[15]

The shields were tacked to the inside of the corset, to reinforce the sides of the waist where the bones were under most stress from bending or stooping, and the packaging promised that they would 'double the life of your corset'. The average corset was only expected to last about a year, as even very sturdy corsets would distort with wear. The Symington Corset Company of Leicestershire guaranteed their corsets for twelve months.

'Oktis' was registered as a company in 1900, but advertisements show that the product was widely available from the late 1890s, and they continued to advertise up until the First World War. Corset shields were sold by the dozen, in two available sizes of four or five blades. These particular shields were made in France by the Oktis Company for import into England, but were also sold under license by the London company of Cook, Son & Co.[16]

'Oktis' corset shield
France, *c*.1900
Calico and steel
V&A: T.431–1985

The "OKTIS" Shiel[d]

Importé d'Angleterre

Supports en Zairolide
ne rouillant pas.

Le fixer en cousant sur les traits......
Ne pas arrêter les extrémités des baleines

OKTIS"
[D]OUBLENT LA DURÉE
DE VOS CORSETS

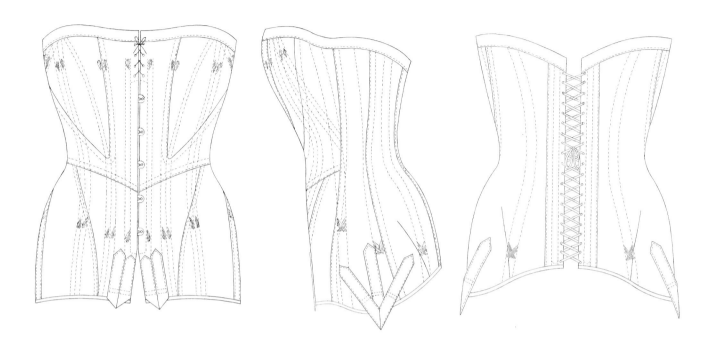

Towards the very end of the nineteenth century, corsetiers introduced straight-fronted corsets as a healthy alternative to the distortions of the 1890s hourglass waist. The most famous of these was the medically trained corsetiere Madame Gâches-Sarrute, who claimed to have invented the style. The idea was that the straight front would not displace the internal organs as the curved busk did. However, the new style – known as the S-bend for the shape it imposed upon the figure – caused a number of new and greater discomforts than the old hourglass style.[17]

The S-bend corset, fashionable between 1900 and 1908, extended much lower than previous corsets, completely enveloping the hips in many cases. The straight-set busk pressed into the groin, which caused the wearer to tilt her hips backwards, arching the back and thrusting the bust forward. A new feature of corsets around this time was integral suspenders, which were attached to the very bottom of the busk to guarantee that the corset was held taut, and to exert a further downward pull on the body. In the case of the corset illustrated here, detached suspender straps were attached to ribbon loops. The corset was still worn over a chemise, combinations or princess petticoat, with any additional petticoat skirts now gathered up and bunched clumsily underneath the suspenders.

Around the turn of the century, high society was characterized by its luxurious and opulent lifestyle. The feminine ideal was one of ampleness, with a figure that showed the signs of lavish consumption and good food. The couturiere Lucile recalled that not one of her fashion models 'weighed under eleven stone, and several of them weighed considerably more. They were big girls with fine figures'.[18] The waist measurement of this corset is a medium to above average size, however the bust measurement shows that the wearer had generous curves that were pushed upwards by the corset, creating the fashionably voluptuous, top-heavy silhouette.

The S-bend was the result of complicated pattern cutting and shaping. There were as many as fifteen separate pieces each side, not including gussets, and it was boned through in different directions with steel and whalebone. In an attempt to alleviate the discomfort of the straight steel busk, a thick white plush lines the inside front of this corset.

Corset
Britain, c.1905
Black silk satin, plush, whalebone and steel
Circumference, bust: 106cm/waist: 62 cm/hip: 98cm
Length front: 53 cm/back: 41 cm
V&A: T.67–1938

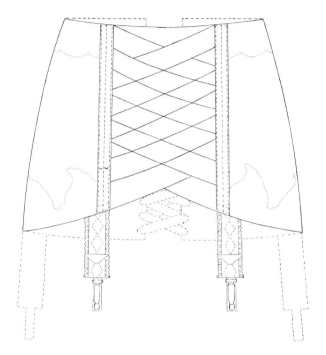
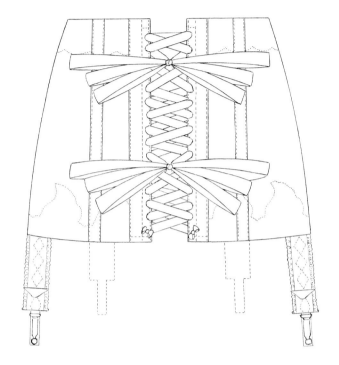

At the beginning of the 1910s a craze for the Tango swept America and Europe, quickly followed by crazes for other frenetic dances such as the Turkey Trot and the Bunny Hug. The vogue for dancing continued up to and during the First World War, and succeeded where decades of dress reformers had failed, by popularizing a reinvented corset style that was less restrictive and more flexible.

The move away from the wasp-waist had been gradual, entering high fashion with couturier Paul Poiret's 1908 collections of long-line draped dresses, with French *Vogue* noting in May of the same year that 'the fashionable figure is growing straighter, less bust, less hips, more waist'. However, the rage for dancing brought the new corset to the general population; by 1913 'Tango Teas' were held regularly in London, and magazines ran regular articles on how to dress for munitions work in the day and for dancing the Tango in the evenings.[19]

By 1914 many young women ridiculed old whalebone corsets, but most needed some kind of foundationwear to achieve the fashionably slim, 'corsetless' figure. Corsets like this one, given names such as 'The Hip-Confiner' or 'Thigh-Diminisher', were introduced to control the buttocks and thighs but permit ease of movement at the upper body.

This corset stretches from the waist to the top of the thighs. It consists of very little boning, except for light channels at the sides and at either side of the metal eyelets. Unusually, the original thick silk lace remains. The front panel of latticed silk satin ribbon allows for up-down movement while retaining tension across its width, delivering both flexibility and a flat stomach. This corset is the direct forerunner of the girdle that would come to dominate foundationwear from the 1920s onwards. It was worn over a petticoat or slip that tucked up underneath the suspenders, and later over shorter cami-knicker sets that developed to better suit this new style (p.54).

'Tango' corset
France (for Debenham & Freebody, London), *c.*1914
Cotton, silk satin ribbon, machine lace, and metal
Circumference, waist: 67cm/hip: 88cm
Length front: 25cm/back: 33cm
Worn and given by Heather Firbank
V&A: T.64–1966

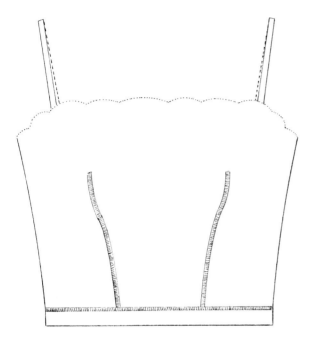
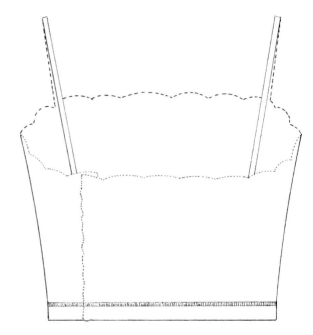

The fashionable figure of the 1900s was statuesque, mature and curvaceous, but the trend in the few years preceding the First World War tended towards a slimmer, younger ideal. The *Journal des Dames et des Modes*, of 10 September 1912, stated: 'At present the thin woman seduces us with her disquieting and alert glamour . . . And youth is *a priori* thin.' During the war, clothing was simplified in order to facilitate manual war work and young women found themselves financially and socially independent for the first time, and so the cult of youth that began before the war increased apace afterwards.

During the 1920s, young people rejected many of the social and moral codes of the elders that led them to war, and expressed their rebellion in their behaviour and appearance.[20] Young women cropped their hair, sported shorter hemlines (just below the knee), wore trousers, and smoked in public. They also flattened their curves, distancing themselves from the matronly figures of the older generation. Dresses were tubular, with long straps and drop-waists that created a straight, relatively androgynous silhouette. Corset companies adapted to cater for the new physical ideal, providing foundation garments – now fashionably dubbed 'girdles' – for women who were not naturally boyish and slim.

Throughout the decade, bandeaux such as this were worn to flatten the bust. This example is made with minimal shaping, from a non-stretch net that helped to compress the breasts. Others were made from firmer materials such as silk-covered rubber, and given names like 'the Reducer'.[21] Bandeaux were worn with a hip-confining girdle, over a slip or camisole. Some featured a narrow tape at the bottom which buttoned to the top of the girdle, pulling the fabric taut to create a straight silhouette from top to bottom. This eventually led to the introduction of the one-piece corselette (p.152).

Bandeau
Britain or France, *c*.1920
Machine-made net with ribbon straps, and hook-and-eye side fastening
V&A: T.195–1967

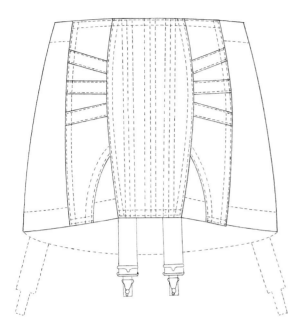

This hook-side girdle is made from sturdy cotton with a satin front panel, half-boned with spiral steels to the mid-point to keep the abdomen flat. Strips of satin radiate from the centre panel to reinforce the front and prevent stretching; it also features panels of an innovative new elastic material called Lastex.

From the 1820s onwards many inventors and companies experimented with ways to develop rubber elastic for clothing.[22] However, it was little used in underwear manufacture during the nineteenth and early twentieth centuries because it was still difficult to source and transport, and could only be produced in short lengths. It also had a tendency to crack and harden. It was used more frequently during the First World War and into the 1920s, when women needed shorter corsets with more flexibility for work and dancing (p.98), but the real technological breakthrough came at the end of the 1920s, when a way was found to export the latex (the sap of the rubber tree from which elastic is made) in liquid form, by adding chemicals such as ammonia.

From this, in 1929, the Dunlop Rubber Company developed a new yarn called Lastex, which could be made longer and finer than previous elastics.[23] It was made by wrapping a fine thread such as cotton or rayon around a core of latex yarn, which could then be woven or knitted into panels with an attractive fabric finish and a two-way stretch ideal for corsetry. Lastex was introduced into general production in the early 1930s, dramatically reducing the need for boning and lacing, and allowing a diversification of styles. 'Roll-ons' were tube-like girdles woven entirely from Lastex that rolled on over the hips without fastenings. 'Step-ins' opened part of the way with hooks and eyes or zips, while 'wrap-arounds' like this opened completely and fastened at one hip (p.136).

In an article entitled 'Practical Underwear', *The Times* of 4 March 1931 states: 'It is on the successful fit of the corset that the success of a gown or costume depends. There are endless varieties of corset . . . designed for the slim and the heavy . . . Rubber corsets . . . are now sometimes made . . . But elastic is more used to-day in combination with satin, moire, or batiste for corsets . . . A corset specialist recommends all women to have four corsets – one for games, one for everyday wear, one (very brief and supple) for rest at home, and one for evening.'

Wrap-around girdle
Excelsior
Britain, 1930s
Cotton, knit rayon elastic (Lastex) and satin, with flat steel boning, hook-and-eye fastenings and integral suspenders
Circumference, waist: 69cm/hip: 86cm
Length, front: 28cm/back: 32cm
Given by Mr Ian Chipperfield
V&A: T.168–1998

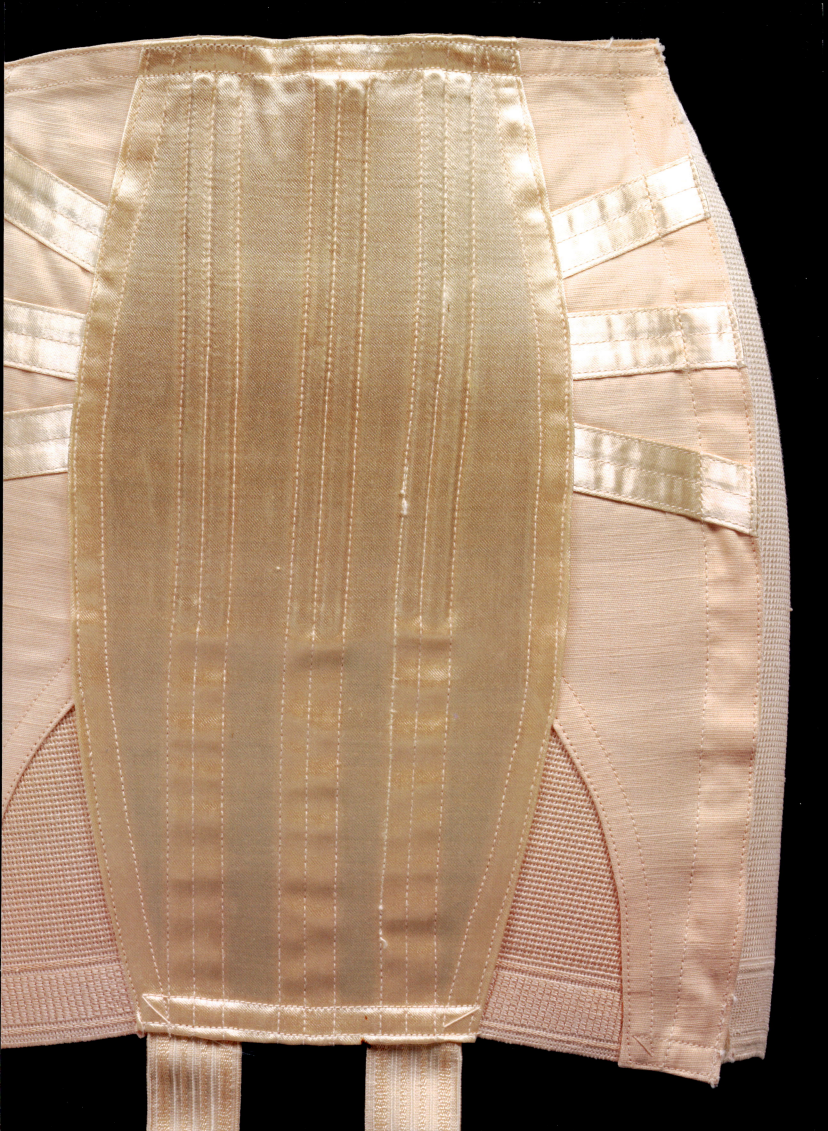

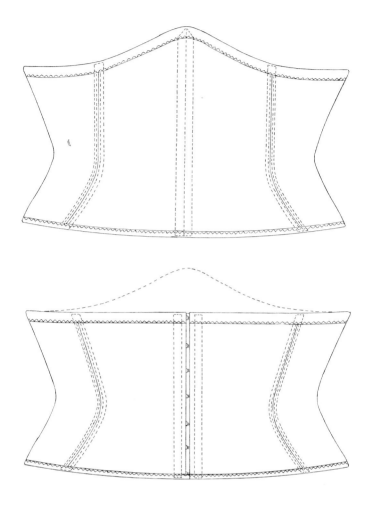

At the end of the 1930s, and with the Second World War looming, fashion indulged in nostalgia. The 1930s had been a decade of slinky bias-cut gowns over firm but fairly naturally proportioned foundations, but 1939 saw the tentative return of both the crinoline and the wasp-waist to the pages of fashion magazines. *The Times* of 12 May that year reported that 'although the modern woman depends to a great extent upon diet and exercise to keep her slim, youthful figure, the sudden return to the small waists and curved hips of our grandmother's time makes careful corsetry a necessity'. The wasp-waist had no time to reinstate itself in popular consciousness, however, before the outbreak of war slowed or stalled fashion's trajectory for the duration of the conflict.

After the war, the nipped-in waist returned, featured in designs by couturiers Robert Piguet, Jacques Fath and Marcel Rochas. The foundation garment that supported this silhouette was different in both name and appearance from the now-antiquated whalebone corset. It was a waist-cinching belt only 10cm deep, known as a *'guêpière'* or 'waspie', and by March 1946 *Harper's Bazaar* was reporting: 'Today every smart little waist knows the tugging, hugging security of it.' In the spring of 1947, Christian Dior secured the waspie's popularity by giving it a central role in the creation of his 'New Look' collection. In 1948, the trade magazine *Le Corset de France* declared the ideal waist size to be 20 inches; in 1929 the ideal had been 29 inches.

During a time of post-war shortages, the waspie was quite an economical use of materials, maximizing its impact at the waist with boning and elastics, and with new materials such as nylon.

This waspie was made by J. Roussel. The company were based in Paris, but also had two branches in London and around Britain in Birmingham, Bristol, Liverpool, Manchester and Glasgow. They specialized in control-wear and were popular from the late 1920s for their corselettes, girdles and bras (p.150).

Waspie
J. Roussel of Paris
France (for British market), 1948
Elasticized cotton, boning, hook-and-eye closure
Waist circumference: 65cm
Length, front: 19cm
Given by P. Wilson
V&A: T.110–2001

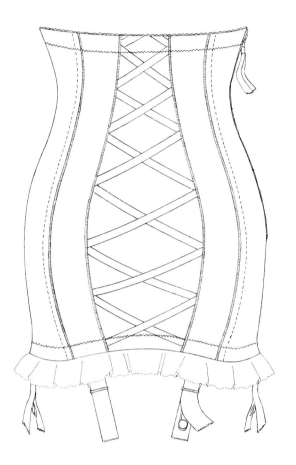

Christian Dior's 'New Look' collection of spring 1947 transformed the fashionable silhouette overnight. The military, boxy styles of the war were replaced by Dior's nostalgic femininity of sloping shoulders, full skirts, padded hips and wasp-waists. Complicated foundations were central to Dior's designs; he relied heavily on waspies, girdles, and horsehair padding, in addition to boning and stiffened net petticoats. Dior's popularity throughout the 1950s guaranteed a market for foundationwear, and sales of corsets doubled in the decade 1948–58.[24]

In 1957, the Symington Corset Company of Market Harborough won the British contract to produce ready-to-wear foundation garments for Christian Dior, who licensed production of various accessories and cosmetics to companies around the world. Symington produced corselettes and girdles for Dior, which sold in luxury shops such as Harrods. All the girdles were produced to the same design, in either black or white. The sugar-pink cotton velvet trimming was a particular feature of the range, and some were woven with Christian Dior's initials in the elastic panels on the side, though

not this model. A 1959 advertisement for the full corselette version reads: 'This exquisite Dior corselet features jacquarded elastic net with down-stretch back panel of satin elastic. The enchanting front panel is in Bri-Nylon lace and marquisette highlighted with criss-cross bands of narrow velvet ribbon. It has side fastening – partly hook and eye with zip extension. The very light boning is covered with velveteen.'[25] The modernity of the range was demonstrated by the advertisement's trumpeting of the very new 'Bri-Nylon' fabric, introduced by British Nylon Spinners towards the end of the 1950s. It was highly popular as it was one of the first easy-to-launder, drip-dry fabrics.

The range was launched at the Savoy Hotel in September 1957, in the same month as Christian Dior's death. The range was, unusually for Dior, not a great seller. At £8, the girdle was expensive, and in 1959 Symington transferred production to the smaller subsidiary company of Alcock & Priestly Ltd. This girdle was part of a large donation of underwear to the V&A that comprised the unsold stock of a high-end London lingerie shop when it closed down.

'Colette' girdle
R. & W.H. Symington & Co. Ltd, under licence from Christian Dior, Paris
Britain (Leicestershire), 1957–9
Elastic net and nylon, satin elastic back panel, with machine nylon lace and cotton velvet
Circumference, underbust: 71cm/waist: 67cm/hip: 91cm
Length front: 46cm/back: 50cm
Given by Caroline Wren
V&A: T.140–2000

This corselette, entitled the 'Seductress', was advertised in the March 1959 edition of French fashion magazine, *L'Officiel*. The advertisement reads that it will make the wearer 'more graceful, more feminine than ever', and will ensure a 'young and slender outline' and a high bosom. It was made in 1959 by Simone Pérèle, who established her corsetry business in Paris in 1948. She believed that women should not have to sacrifice comfort for elegance, and became famous for creating foundationwear using lingerie materials such as French lace. The advent of new highly tensile nylon elastic nets in the 1950s brought about a revolution in underwear design and manufacture, offering powerful control without the need for much boning. It allowed underwear designers such as Pérèle to use a lace effect not only as a decorative trim, but as the garment's primary material – the lace pattern having been woven into the nylon net itself.

This is a version of the 'Merry Widow' corset, named for the 1952 film of the same name starring Lana Turner. In the film, Turner wears several waist-cinching strapless corsets, heavily trimmed with lace. The 'Merry Widow' name was registered by the American company Warner's, who timed the launch of the range with that of the film, and extensively advertised the brand from the mid-1950s to the early 1960s. It was designed to smooth the hips and reduce the abdomen, while also lifting the bust. The 'Merry Widow' name was so popular in America that it became a generic term for any corselette.

The corselette illustrated here features an additional small nylon lace skirt, an ideal foundation for the full-skirted, off-the-shoulder cocktail or evening dresses popular during the late 1950s. The cups are underwired and shaped with a perforated soft rubber foam called lintafoam. It is fastened down the back with eleven hooks and eyes, which are reinforced at each side with a wide panel of nylon power-net to compress the figure.

'Seductress' corselette
Simone Pérèle
France, 1959
Elasticized nylon lace, with lintafoam padding
Circumference, bust: 94cm/waist: 67cm/hip: 91cm
Length, front: 37cm/back: 21cm – neither includes the 14cm of the lace skirt
V&A: T.484–1995

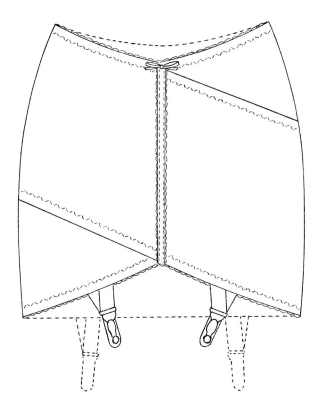
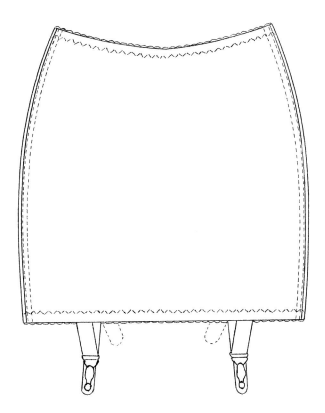

The girdle illustrated here is a 'Little X', made by the British-based firm, Silhouette. The 'Little X' was one of the most successful foundation garments of the 1950s. It was launched in 1955 with a massive advertising budget, funded with credit and bank loans at great risk for the relatively small Silhouette company, who were hoping to reach an emerging youth market with a large-scale American-style advertising campaign. The advertisement was based upon a picture of a young girl, her body in silhouette apart from the highlighted girdle, jumping in an 'X' shape. It showed the girdle stretched to its extreme, to show its elastic qualities and the flexibility it could afford. The campaign ran in cinemas and magazines and was a great success. Turnover was hugely increased, and demand was such that the license to produce the 'Little X' was granted to 32 countries.[26]

Before the mid-1950s, rubber and latex girdles only stretched horizontally and constantly rode up. In 1955 the 'Little X' was the first fully elasticized, brand-name foundation garment marketed in Britain. Initially it used elasticized nylon, but became one of the first garments to incorporate Lycra. It is a completely synthetic stretch fabric, three times more powerful than previous elastics with twice the recovery power. It became increasingly popular throughout the 1960s and is the staple underwear textile today.

The 'Little X' was offered in a variety of bright colours, trimmed with gold lurex. The crossed panel at the front ensured that the hips and buttocks were compressed, while providing a double layer of Lycra over the abdomen to ensure a flat stomach. Because of its tensile strength and stretch, there was no need for boning or for hooks and eyes; it was just rolled on and off – hence the style's popular nickname, 'roll-on'.

'Little X' girdle
Silhouette
Britain, early 1960s
Lycra and nylon, lurex trim, with metal suspender clasps
Circumference, waist: 52cm/hip: 63cm
Length, front: 22cm/back: 29cm
V&A: T.291–1993

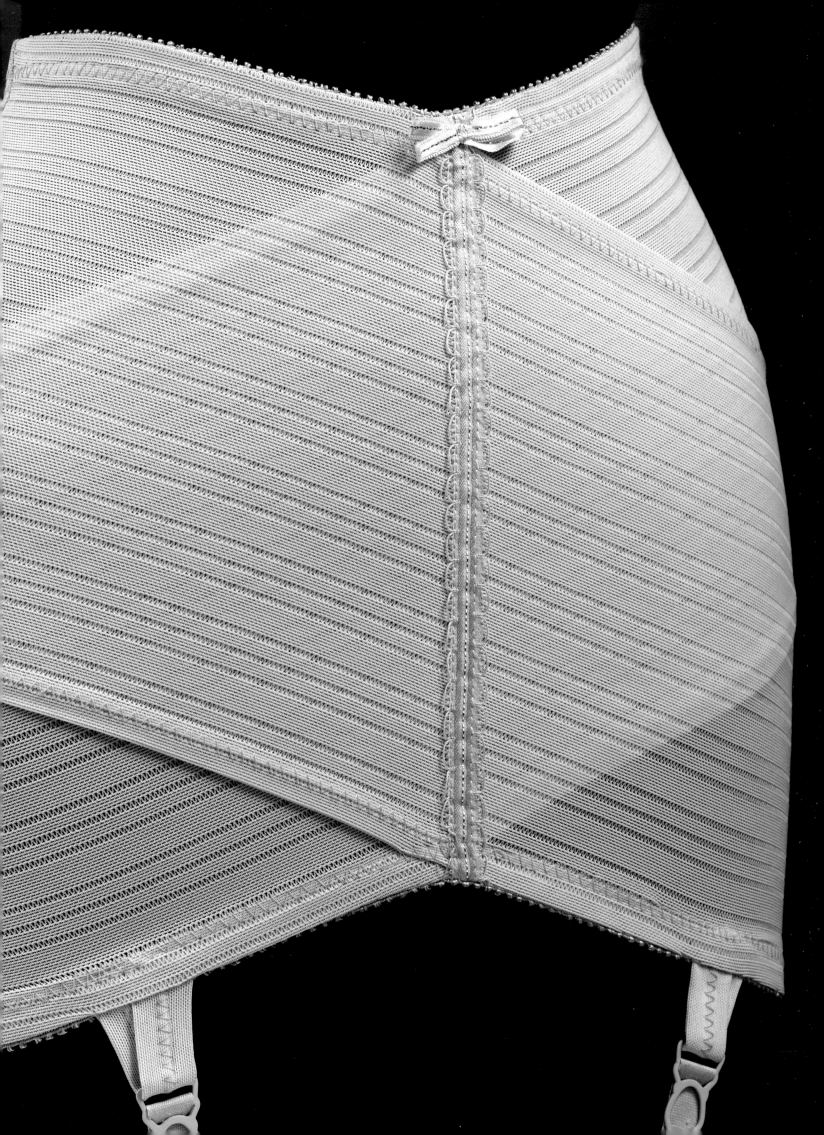

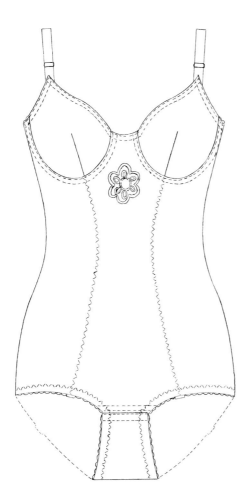
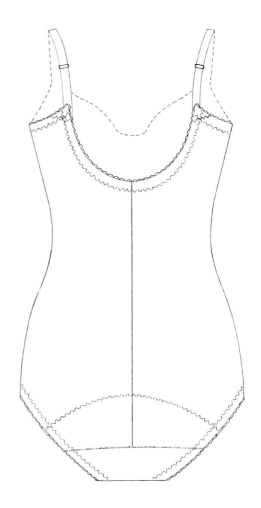

In 1955, Mary Quant opened Bazaar, a small boutique on the King's Road in London that sold ready-to-wear garments designed for an emerging youth market. Within the decade Mary Quant was a global brand.

Quant played an important part in what *Vogue* magazine's editor-in-chief, Diana Vreeland, dubbed the 'youthquake' of the 1960s[27], when young people rebelled against the intellectual and social models of their parents' generation through political activism, music and clothing. Fashion was focused on androgynous adolescent figures like that of model Twiggy, and teenagers looked with derision upon the tea-rose, steel busks and suspenders of the 1950s. When Quant championed the miniskirt, she signalled a change in underwear styling, such as the introduction of tights and streamlined foundation garments that would not show under short skirts and tight tops. Corselettes and girdles continued to be made for the more mature or fuller-figured women, but the popular market and fashionable press largely promoted the new style.

The fashion ethos emanating from 'swinging London' was supported by the innovations in man-made textiles, which provided easy-care fabrics with high-tensile properties that could shape the figure without boning. This bodysuit is made of Lycra, with sheer nylon marquisette cups. A central panel is reinforced with additional layers of Lycra to keep the abdomen flat. The desired effect was a sleek and streamlined silhouette, free from the bulging clasps and zips of traditional girdles, though it does have discreet attachments for optional suspenders.

Quant introduced this underwear range in 1965, branded 'Youthlines Q Form by Mary Quant'. It advertised its use of 'girl loving Lycra', that made the wearer 'all girl' not 'all garment', and boasted that 'even the daisies give'.[28] Mary Quant's daisy logo was used prominently on all garments in this range. The panty-girdle version featured a daisy on each buttock.

Body suit
Mary Quant (b. 1934)
Britain (London), *c.*1965
Synthetic jersey with Lycra, with nylon marquisette
Bust: 34A cup
Circumference (not stretched), waist: 54cm/hip: 60cm
V&A: T.443–1988

 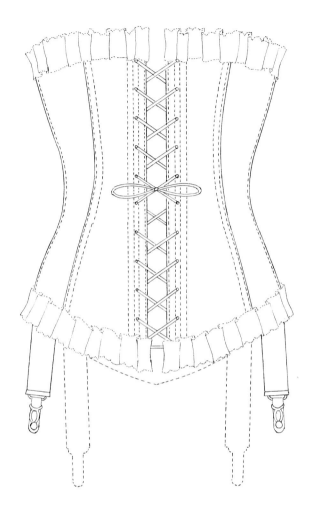

Agent Provocateur was established in 1994 by Joseph Corré and Serena Rees. Originally based in Soho, London, the company expanded rapidly and now has boutiques and department store outlets across the world, running prominent advertising campaigns featuring celebrities and supermodels. The company designs luxury lingerie and corsetry, sold in intimate boudoir-like surroundings.

Corré stated that the couple had wanted their boutique to suggest 'intimacy, glamour, beauty and fashion'. Their main inspiration came from vintage underwear, which they bought up in large quantities to study. Corré explains: 'We started to copy the old stuff, to use old-fashioned fabrics and colours . . . trying to recreate some of these garments, then developed from there into manufacturing.' Corré is the son of fashion designer Vivienne Westwood, and

worked with her for many years, developing her business and brand. However, even given this experience, he was unprepared for the complexities of underwear construction: 'It was a huge culture shock, coming in from the fashion world with Vivienne to making underwear, where you have twenty-four sizes in a single bra and you discover that you need four different types of elastic.'[29]

The corset illustrated here is deliberately reminiscent of late Victorian corsetry (p.126), with its bright colour and traditional corsetry features such as the split metal busk and back lacing. Pink and black are also Agent Provocateur's brand colours. It is cut with a half-cup effect to create a balcony cleavage, boned with fourteen spiral steel bones, and lined with black cotton. It has black elastic integral suspenders with metal clasps.

Corset
Agent Provocateur
Britain (London), late 1990s
Cotton and viscose satin, machine lace with satin ribbon, metal busk, eyelets and spiral steel bones; with cotton lining
Circumference, bust: 84cm/waist: 65cm/hip: 82cm
Length, front: 31cm/back: 28cm
Given by Anne Steinberg
V&A: T.12–2002

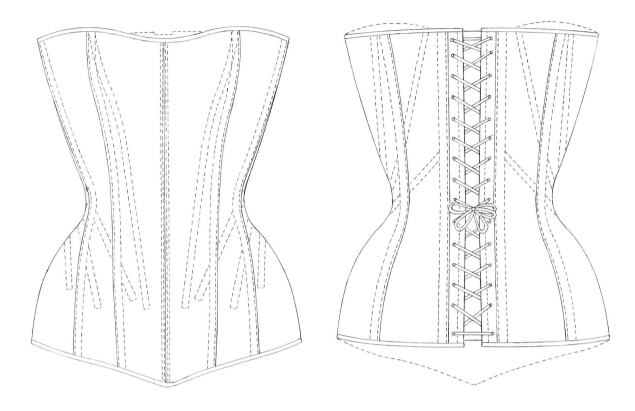

This corset was worn on the catwalk for the presentation of Christian Dior's autumn/winter 2006–7 haute couture collection, designed by John Galliano. It was worn by model Katarina Ivanovska, underneath a heavily embroidered purple silk crêpe dress. The collection itself was presented against a backdrop of Italianate topiary and played upon ideas of body armour and the Renaissance.

The purpose of this corset is to elongate and flatten the torso, and to create – much as Renaissance stays did – a rigid foundation for the rich fabrics and surface embroidery of the outer garment. It has flat plastic bones running from top to bottom and also diagonally over the hips to accentuate and exaggerate the curve of the hipline. It is a long-line, back lacing corset that laces very tightly to compress the bust and upper body.

The corset was created in a hurry and without many fittings, under the high-pressure conditions of Paris Fashion Week. Model fittings for this particular show ran through the night, as is common, and consequently this corset is not a particularly well-finished example. The satin buckles and pulls at pressure points around the waist where the fabric has been hurriedly pasted to an interlining

and then stitched down. The corset was tacked into the dress with large pink stitches, and a narrow strip of unedged purple crêpe wrapped quickly around the centre top point, where it seems the grey was visible under the neckline.

Mr Pearl is a corsetier who works on Dior's couture shows, amongst others. He explains that creating a corset that fits the body correctly requires a minimum of three fittings, and 'can go up to twelve . . . The fitting is done in a corset toile (plain calico prototype). All the marks are made on this toile. If the alterations are very great, then you make another toile and so it goes on. When the toile fits correctly that's when you work in the chosen fabric'. For a catwalk collection, there is only time for one fitting and one toile. In addition to this the models are laced so tightly and quickly into the corsets – contrary to the slow and incremental adjustments recommended – that many suffer breathlessness. Pearl states: 'This is not correct. To be absolutely poured into a tight corset in three minutes, the reaction of the body is extreme. I've seen girls very stressed backstage due to my work, fainting and so on.'[30]

Corset
Christian Dior
France (Paris), haute couture autumn/winter 2006–7
Satin, plastic bones and buckram, with metal eyelets
Circumference, bust: 83cm/waist: 57cm/hip: 86cm
Length, front: 46cm/back: 43cm
Given by Christian Dior
V&A: T.53:5–2008

FASTENINGS

It is so easy to gain inch by inch of that treacherous silken cord, that [ladies] are not conscious of the effect they are producing; whereas if they were obliged to fasten their corsets by buttoning them in front, they would soon find out how tight they are.

The Young Lady's Friend, 1857[1]

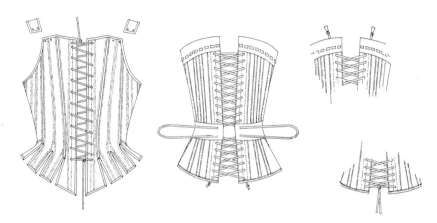

The historical single-lace technique (left), and the post-1843 'lazy lacing' technique (right). Lazy lacing typically employs two laces, but can also be tied with one very long lace; shown here are alternative methods of securing the lace(s) at the top and bottom.[2] Drawings by Matthew Greer.

Before the advent of stretch and elastane fabrics, the process of dressing and undressing relied upon swathes of lacing fastened in increments, and upon a myriad of small ties, clips, clasps, zips, buttons, and hooks and eyes. Dressing was time-consuming and laborious, and necessarily followed a particular order so that all components fitted together correctly.

In *The Edwardians*, Vita Sackville-West describes how Lucy, Duchess of Chevron, 'would rise, and standing in her chemise . . . allow the maid to fit the long stays of pink coutil, heavily boned around her hips and slender figure, fastening the busk down the front after many adjustments; then the suspenders would be clipped to the stockings, then the lacing would follow, beginning at the waist and travelling gradually down . . . The silk laces and their tags would fly out, under the maid's deft fingers, with the flick of a skilled worker mending a net'.[3]

Many technological innovations in underwear fastenings emanate from corsetry construction. Stays were fastened with a single lace in a spiral pattern; they were usually laced at the back and required help to tie. However, in 1843, lacing '*à la paresseuse*' (lazy lacing) was introduced, which allowed the wearer to tighten her own corset. It featured two long loops at waist level that the wearer used to tug the laces tighter herself. The long loops could then be tied around the waist

and tucked neatly under a small hook at the lower front of the corset. Lazy lacing was only made possible by developments in other areas of corset fastening, such as the introduction of the split steel busk and slot-and-stud fastenings, which entered commercial production towards the middle of the nineteenth century.

Historically, tapes, ribbons and laces were the main forms of fastening, holding underwear closed and in place. Simple ribbon or tape garters, for example, were for centuries the only way to hold stockings up. They were worn by both men and women and tied around the leg above the knee, until the arrival of braces for men at the end of the eighteenth century and suspenders for women towards the end of the nineteenth century (p. 134).[4] Suspenders were worn as separate belts or harnesses and, from the beginning of the twentieth century, as integral attachments to the bottom of corsets and girdles. Clipping suspenders onto stockings was a daily routine for women up until the 1960s, when the introduction of tights rendered them largely obsolete apart from occasional or lingerie wear.

In addition to a selection of garters and suspenders, this chapter also includes a collection of twentieth-century girdles which feature hooks and eyes, and fastening innovations such as the zip.

Laces of braided cord and ribbons were the common means of secure fastening for undergarments until the invention of steel clasps in the nineteenth century. These watered silk stays of the 1660s feature front lacing, with ribbon and point ties for detachable silk sleeves that were turned up to form deep cuffs.

Most high-status stays lace at the back, signifying that the wearer had a lady's maid to help her get dressed. However, some stays, such as these, make a feature of decorative front lacing. The eyelets are bound with whip-stitches, and under the lacing is a separate triangular whalebone stomacher, which straightens and flattens the torso and prevents the lacing cutting into the flesh when the wearer moves or sits. The shoulder straps are positioned off the shoulder for a fashionably low neckline; they extend from the back and attach to the front by a loop and ribbon. Attached along the bottom side of the shoulder straps are small chain-stitch thread loops, through which the sleeves are tied to the stays with wide silk grosgrain ribbons. The ribbons still feature their original tinned iron points, designed to make it easier to thread them through the loops. These are rare survivals, as the metal usually rusts away. The sleeves are positioned far back, in accordance with the contemporary bodice style, encouraging an upright posture and forcing the chest forwards.

Throughout the seventeenth century, figure-shaping was achieved with stays or by boning and stiffening the lining of the outer bodice. Stays became firmly established as separate undergarments when the unreinforced manuta gown became fashionable towards the end of the century. In addition, in 1665, Parisian stay-makers were granted permission to establish a guild distinct from traditional tailors, and developed increasingly sophisticated and specialized skills.

Stays with attached sleeves
Britain (probably), 1660s
Watered silk (English or Italian), linen backing, silk thread, and whalebone; with silk grosgrain ribbons
Circumference, bust: 77cm[5]/waist: 49cm/hip: 74cm
Length, front: 40cm/back: 48cm
Given by Miss C.E. Gallini
V&A: T.14&A–1951

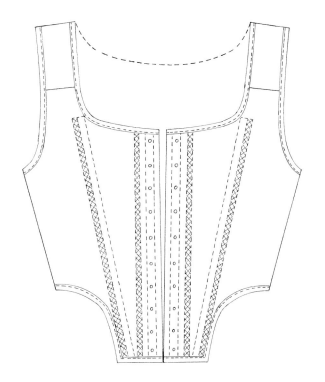

Metal eyelets were introduced in the 1820s. Up until that point, eyelets were bound with stitching in a whip or buttonhole stitch. Sometimes, 'French holes' – small circles of bone, ivory or cording – were stitched into the eyelets for reinforcement, but despite the best efforts, stitched eyelets were easily frayed by the tension and friction of the laces. The eyelets illustrated here are bound with fine buttonhole stitching that shows signs of wear at the stress points where the lace was pulled through, and in some instances the lace has worn through the stitching into the glazed cotton fabric itself. At this time stays and jumps were generally laced from the bottom upwards, with a single lace threaded up through the eyelets in a spiral and tied in a knot at both ends. Eyelets were sometimes off-set so that the lacing pulled the sides together evenly (p.119).

This lightly boned garment is known as a pair of jumps. Jumps were worn as informal stays around the home, often under loose and open-fronted robes. Consequently, many were embellished at the centre-front, or featured decorative front lacing, as this one does. Jumps were also worn for horse riding and for physical work, as they allowed greater mobility than stays.

These jumps are made of glazed cotton and are cut high over the hips and at the back, where they are completely unboned. The two central front panels extend down over the abdomen to the longest point. There are three bones at each side of the front panels – two at either side of the eyelets to help reinforce them and create a straight and flat torso, and one on a diagonal to hint at the fashionable conical shape created by full whalebone stays. Next to two of the whalebone casings are parallel but unboned casings with simple cross-stitch embroidery in a light and dark pink thread. They provide decoration and reinforce the bones, somewhat like the technique of 'flossing' used in the nineteenth century.

Jumps
Britain, 1790–95
Glazed cotton with twill tape, silk thread and whalebone
Circumference, bust: 71cm/waist: 57cm
Length, front: 28cm/back: 22cm
V&A: T.69–1935

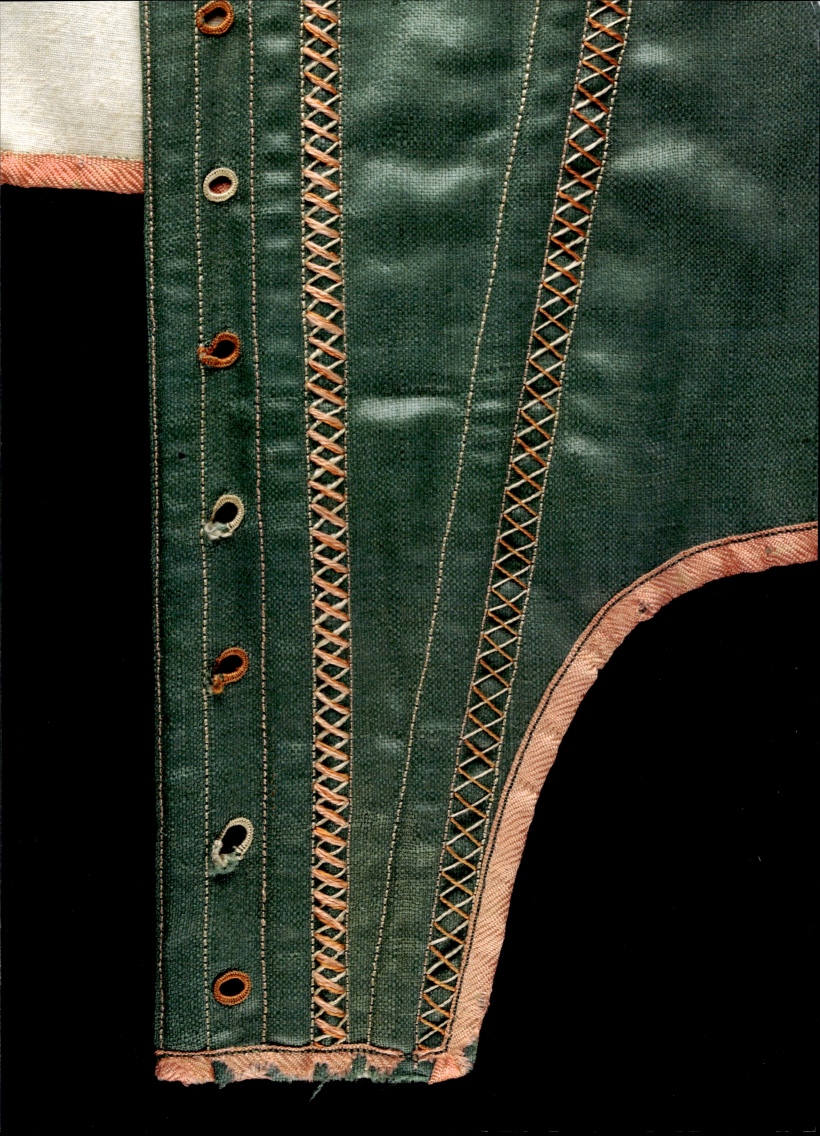

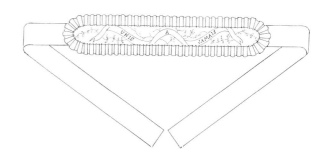

Because garters were hidden, they sometimes carried avowals of love or secret loyalty. Some were amorous, but some were political – possibly even dangerously so. Woven into this garter is the message: 'OUR PRINCE IS BRAVE OUR CAUSE IS JUST'. The prince in question was Charles Edward Stuart, also known as 'Bonnie Prince Charlie', who led a rebellion against King George II to restore the house of Stuart to the British throne. The rebellion was crushed at the battle of Culloden in 1746, but covert support continued for the exiled prince for many years.

Garter
Britain
Woven silk
Given by Miss Ruby Logan in accordance
with the wishes of Miss Evelyn Cooke
V&A: T.121–1931

These garters are made of padded satin, edged with a pleated frill of plain tabby woven ribbon which is also used for the ribbon that ties around the leg. Messages and scrolling rosebuds are embroidered onto the facing with silver and coloured silk thread in chain stitch, reading: 'UNIS A JAMAIS' (united for ever) and 'JE MEURS OU JE M'ATTACHE' (I die where I take root). The latter is a traditional statement of fidelity and is usually shown with winding ivy to symbolize faithful attachment. It is probable that these garters were embroidered and worn for a wedding.

Garter
France, c.1780
Silk satin with embroidered silk
Given by Christopher Lennox Boyd
V&A: T.106&A–1969

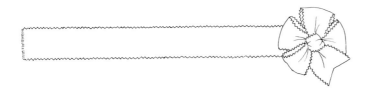

Suspenders were introduced to Britain in the 1870s, notably by the dancers of the Parisian Grand Opera Bouffe, who made the headlines by flashing their suspenders while dancing at the Alhambra Theatre in London.[6] Suspender attachments and belts were worn in small numbers from the 1880s, though it was only at the beginning of the twentieth century that they became integral to corsets and completely replaced garters in general use. Garters, like these elaborate figured silk rosettes, tied over the knee so that the knee-cap could offer another obstacle to prevent the stockings falling down round the ankles. Only with the advent of elasticated fabrics and silicone-grip hold-ups in the 1960s could stockings stay up without the aid of either the garter or suspender clasp.

Garter
British, 1870–1900
Figured silk satin
Given by Messrs Harrods Ltd
V&A: T.1813&A–1913

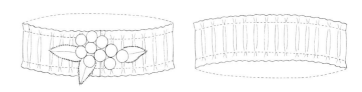

These garters are made of satin, gathered onto black silk grosgrain ribbon and lined with elastic. They feature a bold spray of silk and wire leaves and small padded satin berries. They were designed by Lucile, whose creations were notoriously sumptuous and featured rich fabrics, flowers, fruits and feathers. Though she generally designed clothes in light pastels, she was also given to extravagant flashes of bold colour. As hems shortened towards the end of the 1910s, garters were sometimes worn below the knee as visible accessories to match the rest of the outfit.

Garter
Lucile (Lady Lucy Duff-Gordon, 1863–1935)
Britain (London), c.1920
Satin, grosgrain ribbon and elastic
Worn and given by Heather Firbank
V&A: T.61&A–1960

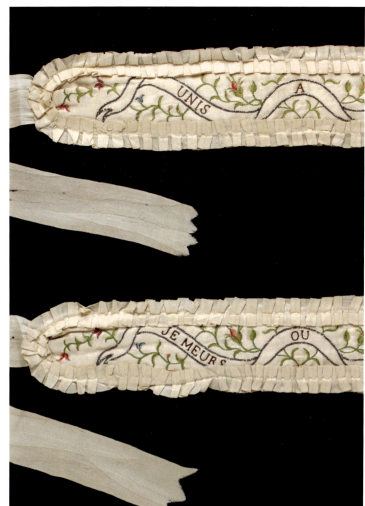

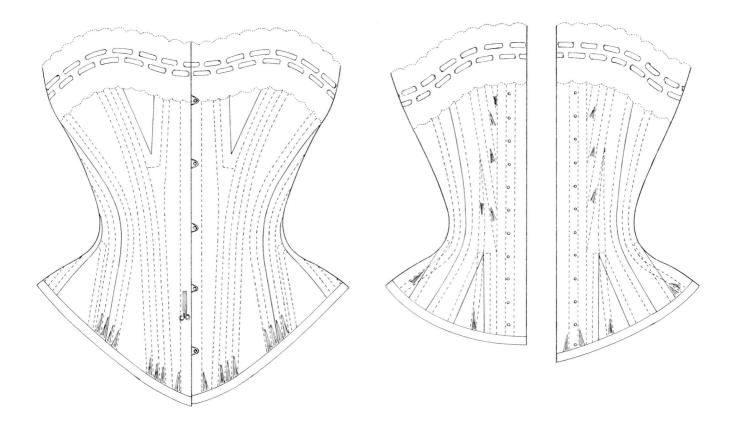

In 1823 Jean-Julien Josselin introduced the first two-part, front-fastening steel busk at the *Exposition Universelle* in Paris.[7] It was fastened with hooks and allowed the wearer to put on and remove the corset without assistance. However, the hooks were not always secure and there were reports of corsets popping open at inopportune moments. Consequently, it was not adopted on a large scale until Joseph Cooper registered a patent for the 'slot-and-stud' fastening in 1848. Combined, the inventions were so efficient that the system was universally adopted after 1850 and is still in use today. Up until this point almost all corsets were laced at the back, with a solid central busk that was inserted into a pocket at the front of the corset (p.76), which meant that help was required to tie on and remove the corset, and that the lace had to be completely removed each time the corset was taken off.

With the 'slot-and-stud' system, the metal slots are fixed to one of the steel busks and the studs to the other. Under tension, the studs pull into the narrow part of the slot and are held securely by the pressure of the body. The two-part steel busk was a much more rigid central force than the whalebone busks of preceding years, which moulded slightly to the body of the wearer when it was warmed by her body heat. Different shapes and styles were tried in order to make the steel busk more comfortable, such as the rounded spoon busk of the 1870s and 1880s that curved over the abdomen, and the straight-fronted busk seen here, which was introduced in the late 1880s. The straight busk was lengthened and exaggerated in the early 1900s, becoming the S-bend corset (p.96). This corset is formed of ten shaped pieces with gussets at the bust and hips and directional rows of whalebone that create an hourglass silhouette. The busk extends over the abdomen for an elongated torso typical of the 1890s.

Colourful satin corsets and petticoats were fashionable in the 1880s and 1890s. Though white was seen as the respectable colour for underwear, visually dramatic undergarments were also seen. *La Vie Parisienne* magazine of 2 May 1885, stated that colourful corsets were: 'Very elegant and extremely becoming. Evidently designed to be seen and . . . looked at!'

Corset
Britain, early 1890s
Silk satin and whalebone, with centre-front steel busk, back lacing with metal eyelets, and hand-made bobbin lace trim
Circumference, bust: 76cm/waist: 50cm/hip: 70cm
Length, front: 31cm/back: 30cm
V&A: T.738–1974

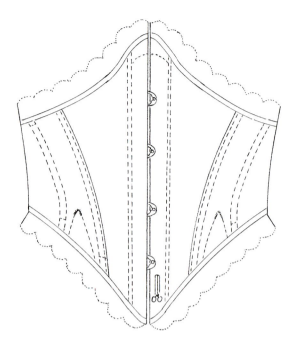

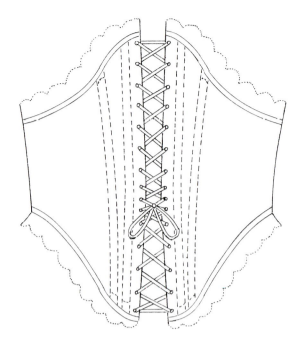

Though small, this corset provides discernible waist cinching, to create a defined hourglass figure. It is lined with cotton coutille and laced at the back through metal eyelets.

Prototype metal eyelets were registered by Rogers of London in 1823, but modern stamped metal eyelets, as seen here, were registered by Daude of Paris in 1828.[8] Before this, eyelets were reinforced with stitching (p.122), or more rarely with small hoops of bone known as 'French holes'. Metal eyelets were stamped down over the edges of the punched cloth, requiring no stitching. They reinforced the fabric holes, allowing the corset to be laced quicker and tighter. Around 1840, as a natural consequence of these new metal eyelets that could withstand higher levels of friction, a lacing technique known as 'à la paresseuse' or 'lazy lacing' was devised (p.119). The metal eyelets were spaced closer together at the waist, showing where the loops should be positioned and offering further reinforcement against the stress of the tugging laces.

This corset style was advertised throughout the 1890s as a 'Swiss belt', 'riding corset' or 'bicycle waist'. It is cut high over the hips and low under the bust, to allow easy movement for the popular ladies' pastimes of horse riding or bicycling, and for other fashionable sports like croquet or golf. *The Ladies Home Journal* of August 1896 advertised the versatility of the belt corset, stating that it made its wearer 'graceful all the time' whether 'at work, a-wheel, [or] in negligee'.

Swiss belt corset
Britain, 1890s
Silk satin lined with cotton coutille, with whalebone, centre-front steel busk,
back lacing with metal eyelets, and broderie anglaise trim
Waist circumference: 66cm
Length, front: 28cm/back: 28cm
Given by Messrs Harrods Ltd
V&A: T.912–1913

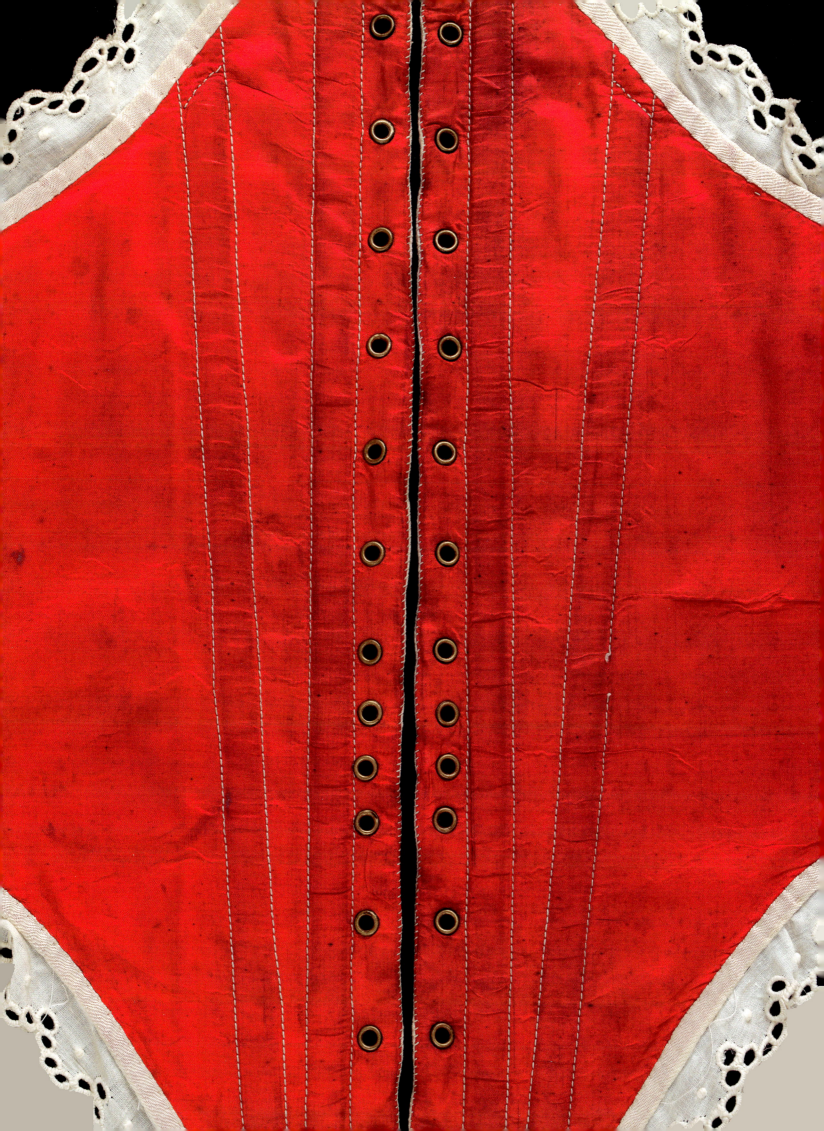

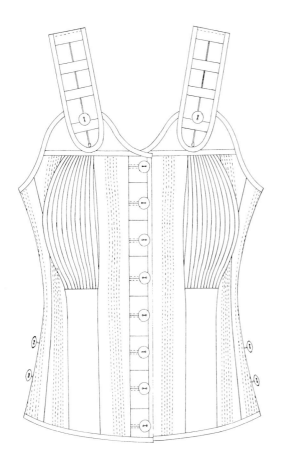
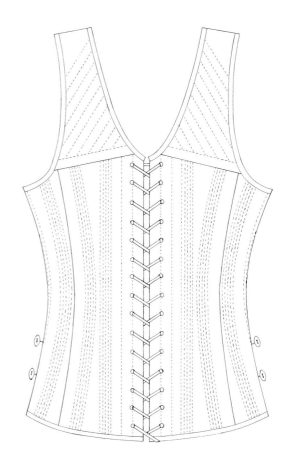

In 1878 Dr Gustav Jaeger published a collection of essays based on ten years of study as Professor of Zoology and Physiology at the University of Stuttgart. His essays advocated wearing only wool next to the skin, claiming that vegetable fibres such as cotton or linen weakened the body by cooling the skin too quickly and absorbing the body's noxious vapours, thereby keeping them too close to the body. Wool, he argued, ensured proper ventilation and warmth. In 1884 his essays were translated into English, and in the autumn of that year he won a gold medal at the International Health Exhibition, held in London under the auspices of the Rational Dress Society. The same year, via his London-based licensee, Lewis Tomalin, he introduced a full range of woollen clothing and underwear marketed as the 'Jaeger Sanitary Woollen System'.[9]

In the 1880s and 1890s, dress reformers campaigned vigorously against the perceived dangers of wearing whalebone corsets. In published pamphlets, books and public lectures, the corset was blamed for a host of diseases and deformities, from punctured lungs and broken ribs to uterine disorders and birth abnormalities.

Dr Jaeger, however, said that the fault did not lie wholly with the corset but with the material from which it was made, saying that a 'sanitary woollen corset' encouraged strong healthy bodies that would not require the support of steel and whalebone.[10]

The Jaeger corset bodice illustrated here is made of finely woven unbleached wool, with ribs of twisted wool cording, knife-pleated bust sections, and woollen twill tape edging. It still features traditional back lacing, allowing the corset to be tightened and adjusted. However, it has a button fastening at the front and wide shoulders straps that were much favoured by dress reformers.

This model was designed for teenage girls, whose healthy physical development was a key issue for dress reformers and health campaigners; mothers were urged to opt for 'rational' and 'good sense' corset bodices for their daughters. There are several buttonholes along the shoulder straps, allowing for easy adjustment as the wearer grew, and for general comfort and fit. Corset bodices were also introduced for adult women, and were believed particularly appropriate for maids as they offered support with flexibility.

Corset bodice
Jaeger Sanitary Woollen System
Britain, 1890s
Wool, with woollen cording, braid lacing and twill tape; with mother-of-pearl buttons and nickel eyelets
Circumference, bust: 74cm/waist: 59cm/hip: 68cm
Length, front: 32cm/back: 31cm
Given by Miss E.J. Bowden
V&A:T.229–1968

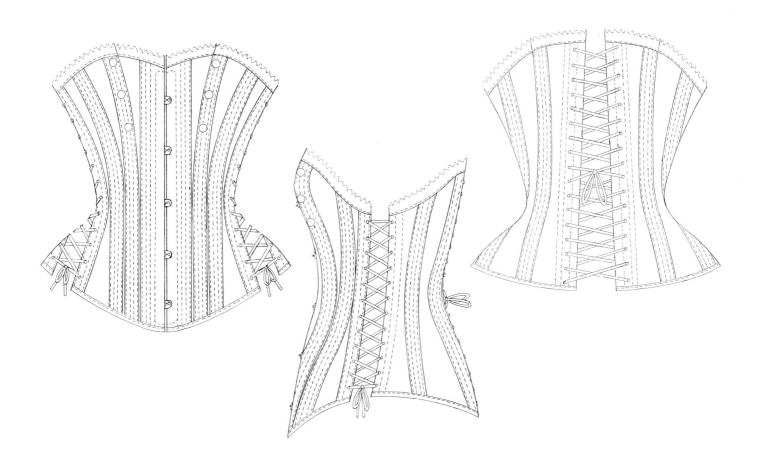

Until the twentieth century, stays and corsets were worn throughout pregnancy. Like ordinary corsets, they were boned with rigid busks running down the centre-front, but they made a concession to pregnancy with the addition of side laces that could be adjusted to accommodate a swelling belly.

Doctors and dress reformers denounced the use of corsets during pregnancy, directly attributing infant mortality to their use and the pressure they exerted on the uterus.[11] However, received wisdom – via magazine articles, advertisements and general social mores – warned that without suitable corsetry, the abdomen and uterus would become stretched and unsupported.

Many patents for 'safe' maternity corsets were advertised towards the end of the nineteenth century, but still more focused on how women could achieve a slim waist as soon as possible after childbirth,

especially considering that most women endured repeated and frequent pregnancies. An expanded waist was the opposite of the fashionable ideal, and the London corsetiere Madame Roxey Caplin promoted corsets that banished the 'baneful consequences resulting from gestation'.[12] She acknowledged that some maternity corsets were badly made, but defended her craft, claiming that: 'It never seems to have occurred to the Doctors that ladies must and will wear stays . . . [for they] desire to retain as long as possible the charm of beauty and the appearance of youth.'[13]

This corset is made in four parts, from a now-grubby cotton twill, trimmed at the top with machine-embroidered tape. At each breast are openings for breast-feeding, kept closed with press studs, showing that these corsets were also for post-natal use, allowing for nursing while helping the figure back to its pre-pregnancy shape.

Maternity/nursing corset
Britain or Germany, c.1900
Cotton twill with centre-front steel busk, side and back lacing, metal eyelets and bronze gilt press studs,
with machine-embroidered trim
Circumference, bust: 77cm/waist: 53cm/hip: 77cm
All the above measurements include the extant 3cm of adjustable lacing at each side (narrowing to 2cm at the bust)
Length, front: 34cm/back: 33cm
Given by the family of Mayer Yanovsky
V&A: T.98&A–1984

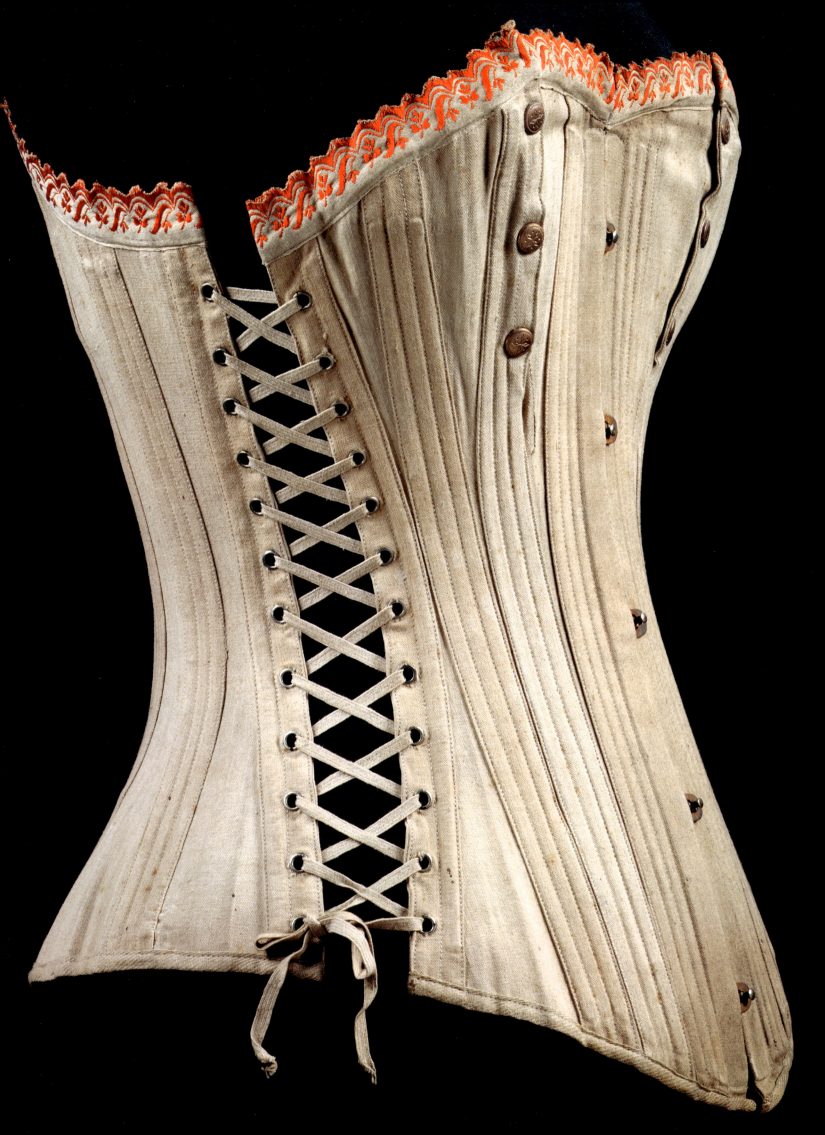

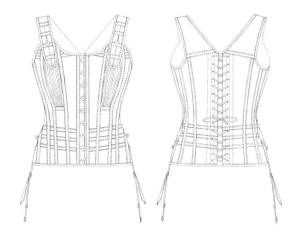

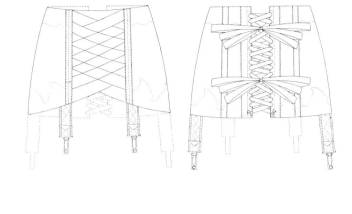

From the 1880s, rational style corset bodices often featured buttons at the hips, stitched in a diamond pattern, as seen here. After putting on her chemise and corset, the wearer attached the suspenders to her stockings, next buttoning her drawers to the lower button, and finally securing her petticoat to the top buttons before dressing in her outer garments.

Corset bodice
Britain, *c*.1900
Cotton with mother-of-pearl buttons and metal suspender clasp
Circumference, bust: 86cm/waist: 70cm/hip 80cm
Length, front: 34cm/back: 34cm
V&A: T.236–1989

Suspenders were commonly attached to the bottom of corsets from the beginning of the twentieth century. During the fashion for S-bend corsets, suspenders were attached to the bottom of the busks to create a straight and taut line from bust to thigh, but later, during the dancing craze of the 1910s, corsets were required to allow more movement and flexibility and suspenders were positioned to the sides, like this, to allow the legs to kick out. Suspenders served the dual purpose of holding stockings in place and preventing the corset from riding up. Also see p.98.

'Tango' corset
France (for Debenham & Freebody, London), *c*.1914
Cotton, silk satin ribbon, machine lace, metal and rubber
Worn and given by Heather Firbank
V&A: T.64–1966

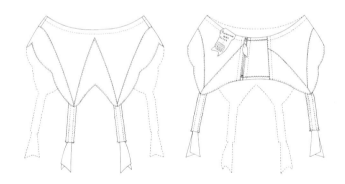

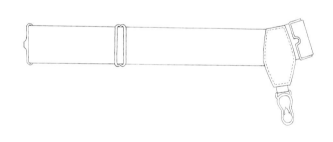

This is an example of a fashionable and youthful suspender belt that anticipates the vibrant designs of the 1960s. The introduction of nylon into the commercial market in the 1950s helped to diversify the kinds of fabrics and finishes available, and innovations in printing and colour techniques put an end to the thirty-year dominance of tea-rose pink for underwear. Bright floral prints such as this became popular with stylish young women, as *Punch* magazine of 16 March 1955 exclaimed: 'There is no pink – not in Paris.'

Suspender belt
Corsets Charmereine
France (Paris), late 1950s
Nylon, with nylon power net, elastic, and rubber and metal clasps
Given by Caroline Wren
V&A: T.144:2–2000

From the 1880s to the introduction of Lycra in the early 1960s, sock suspenders were a standard underwear support. Most men wore sock suspenders in order to prevent their socks falling down and bunching around their ankles. They were worn at the top of the calf, just under the knee, with the clasp at the front of the leg.

These sock suspenders are a typical design: made of a wide elasticated band, with a piece of leather through it to reinforce and hold the brass and rubber clasp. There is a brass fitting to one side so that the elastic can be adjusted.

Sock suspender
Britain, *c*.1950
Elastic, brass and rubber
V&A: T.852&A–1974

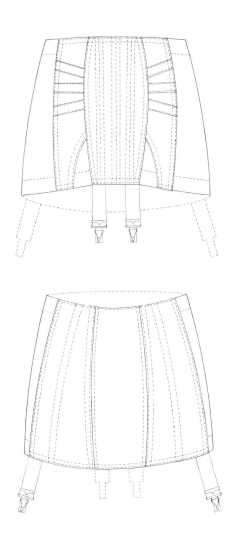

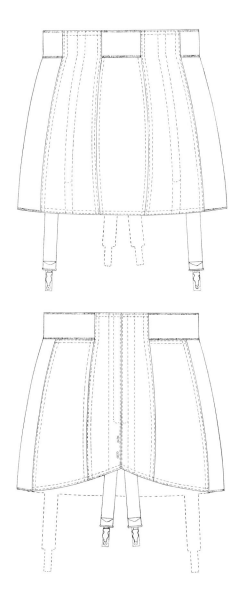

This hook-side girdle wraps around the hips and fastens with hooks and eyes at the left side. This method of fastening was much used in the 1930s as it was less bulky than other types of fastening and afforded a smooth silhouette under the slinky, bias-cut dresses of the decade. The integral suspenders serve not only to hold up the wearer's stockings, but also to anchor the girdle down and prevent it riding up. To reduce bulk further, girdles were worn without a slip underneath for the first time. Also see p.102.

Wrap-around girdle
Excelsior
Britain, 1930s
Cotton, rayon elastic and satin, with flat steel boning,
hook-and-eye fastenings and integral suspenders
V&A: T.168–1998

During the Second World War, innovation in underwear design slowed. This wrap-around girdle was first launched in 1932 and was modified only slightly during the war to comply with the strict rules of the government Utility Scheme, established to ration materials and control standards. It features a centre-front split steel busk with a slot-and-stud fastening, itself unchanged since its introduction in the middle of the nineteenth century. Inside the girdle is a printed label marked 'CC41', which identifies it as a product of the Utility Scheme by the abbreviation of its full name, the 'Civilian Clothing Act of 1941'. The colour of this, and other girdles shown here and on the following page, is 'tea-rose', the standard colour for foundation garments from the early 1930s into the 1950s.

'Avro' wrap-around girdle
R. & W.H. Symington
Britain (Leicestershire), 1942–9
Cotton broche with rayon elastic panels, flat steel bones
and slot-and-stud busk
Circumference, waist: 64cm/hip: 89cm
Length, front: 29cm/back: 34cm
V&A: T.170–1998

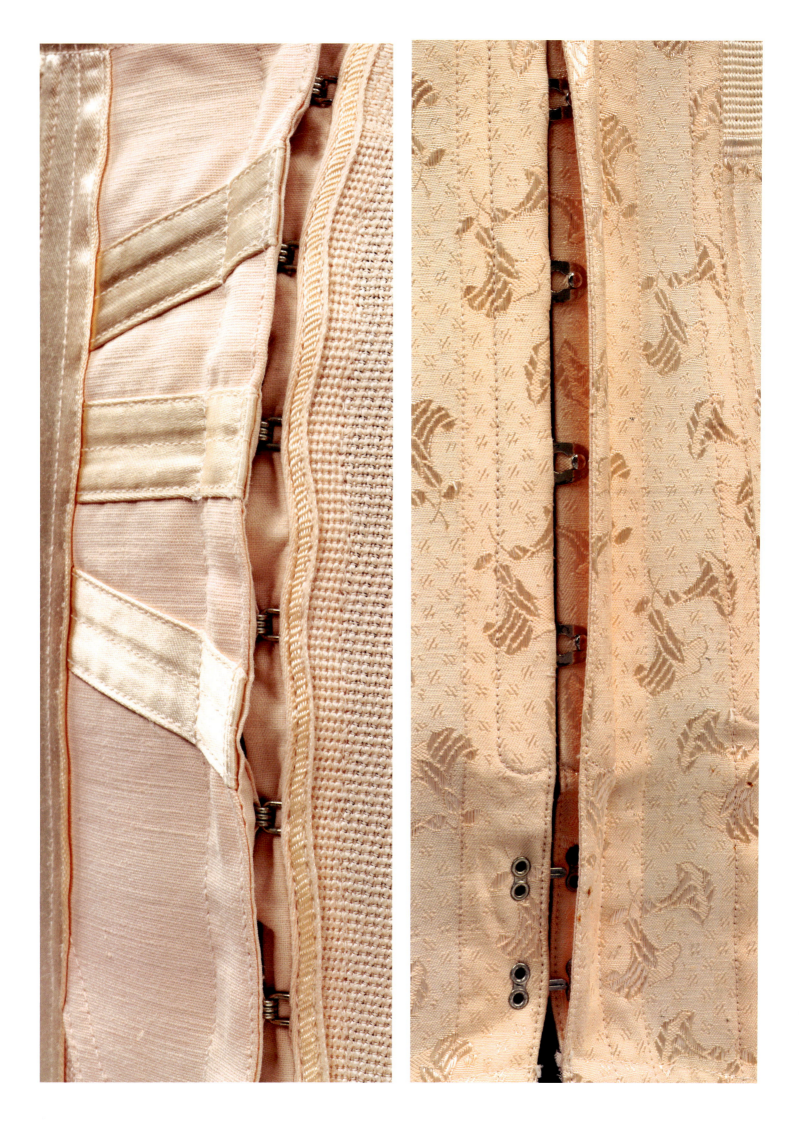

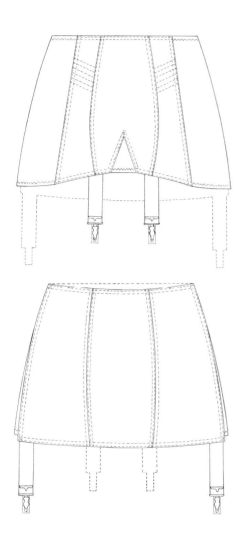

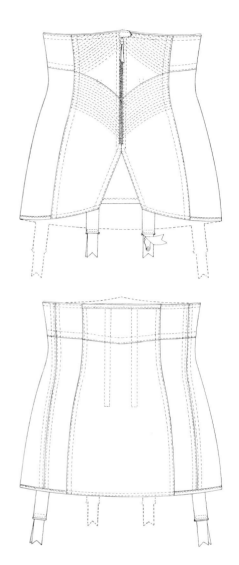

During the Second World War, most corset factories, their employees and their materials were drafted into the war effort. However, it seems that the women of Britain could do without many things – except good-quality girdles. In 1943, the Corset Guild of Britain presented a petition to the government stating that physical work demanded good physical support, and on 21 March 1944, the President of the Board of Trade assured Parliament that he had 'arranged for increased production of the strongest utility corset cloths', considering it essential for health and morale.[14] However, steel for fastenings was in exceptionally short supply towards the end of the war – necessary, as it was, to make armaments – and so girdles were made to contain as little steel as possible. The interior of this girdle demonstrates the careful use of reinforcing fabric panels and minimal use of steel.

Wrap-around girdle
Britain, 1940s
Rayon satin and elastic, hook-and-eye fastenings and
integral suspenders
Circumference, waist: 65cm/hip: 92cm
Length, front: 27cm/back: 31cm
V&A: T.300–1993

In 1951, the lingerie designer Miss Marene wrote *The Production of Modern Lingerie*, in which she states that 'recently, people have begun using such a thing as a zipp'.[15] Though various forms of zip fastenings were registered for patents as early as 1851, they received little attention from the fashion industry until the 1930s, and the war effectively put paid to its mass commercial use until the end of the 1940s. Here, the zip is used as a streamline fastening for a high step-in girdle that cinches the waist for the fashionable 1950s hourglass shape.

Step-in girdle
Britain, early 1950s
Nylon satin, with elasticized nylon net, zip fastening and
integral suspenders
Circumference, waist: 71cm/hip: 91cm
Length, front: 38cm/back: 43cm
V&A: T.138–2000

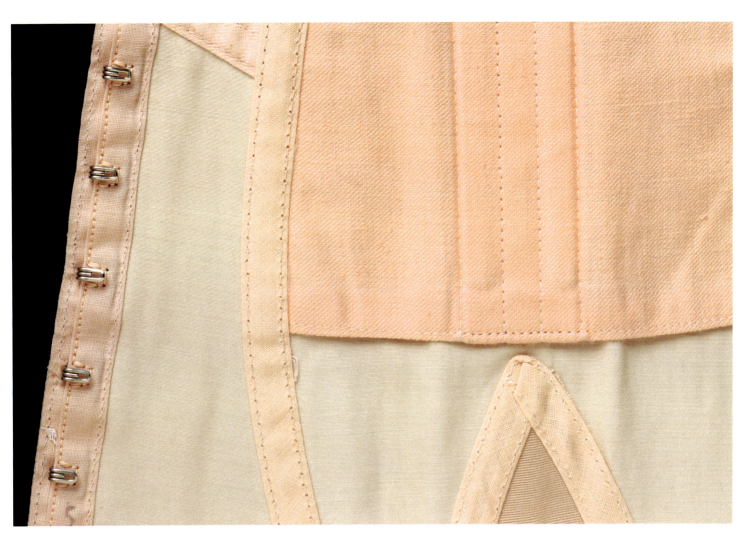

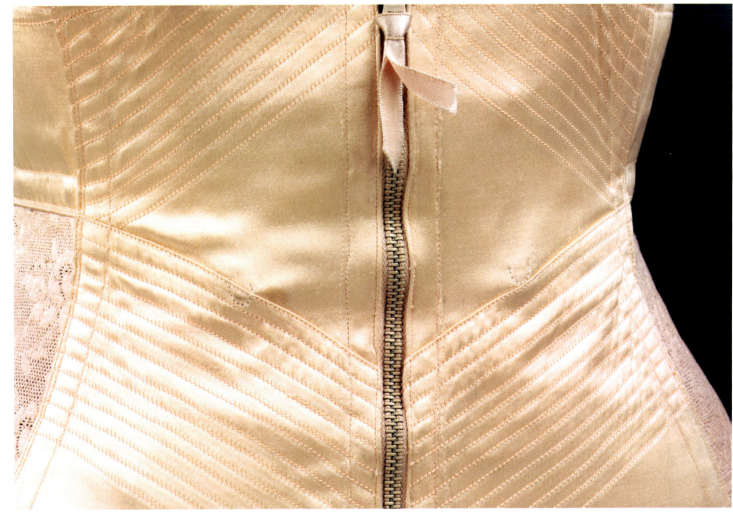

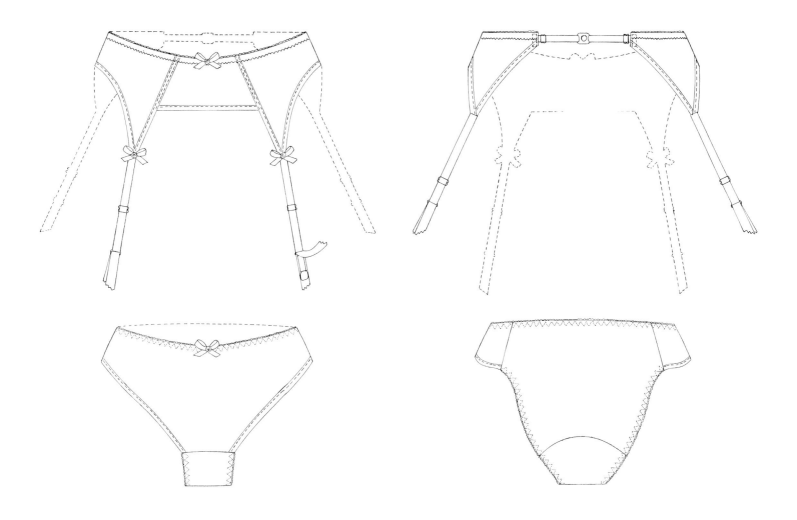

Suspender belts were introduced in the 1870s, designed as separate garments to wear over the corset. By the beginning of the twentieth century they were usually attached to the bottom of corsets and later to girdles. They remained a common feature of foundation garments into the 1960s, when the invention of tights and elastane (spandex) rendered them obsolete. Suspenders were subsequently seen only on the most traditional ranges, and by 1980 stocking sales accounted for only 6 per cent of the hosiery market.[16]

Suspender belts and stockings are now generally seen as sexy, seductive items. They allude to a time when undressing was a slow and complicated procedure, hindered by the clasps, fastenings and ties of corsets, girdles and belts. They add retro-glamour to modern undressing, and an element of performance. Throughout the 1990s and early 2000s, burlesque shows were popular and stars like Dita Von Teese and Immodesty Blaize became mainstream celebrities, famous for their 1940s and 1950s image and use of vintage aesthetics such as suspenders and waist cinchers.

This racy red tulle and satin lingerie set includes a suspender belt, with clear plastic clips under satin ribbons, to hold up the matching red nylon stockings. The transparent tulle is accented with black rosettes and red satin ribbon. The ensemble deliberately references 1950s pin-up imagery, with a drawing on the stockings packet showing a curvaceous, reclining woman wearing the ensemble and lighting a cigarette from the lit fuse of a bomb.

This ensemble is typical of Agent Provocateur's designs. It is overtly risqué, but is packaged and marketed as an indulgent luxury item. Agent Provocateur was established in 1994, selling expensive, erotic lingerie, and quickly became a global brand and market-leader for other lingerie boutiques. The UK lingerie market grew by 19 per cent between 2003 and 2008[17], with the greatest increase recorded by high-end lingerie retailers such as Agent Provocateur.

Suspender belt
Agent Provocateur
France (for retail in Britain), 1999
Polyester and nylon mix tulle with satin ribbon and rosettes, with plastic clips
Given by Agent Provocateur
V&A: T.870&1–2000

SUPPORT AND UPLIFT

Even if she has the right amounts of fashion flair and cash
to aspire to the lists of the best-dressed,
the woman with the wrong amount of bosom will never make it.

Time, 29 June 1962

The brassiere is a relatively recent invention, for historically breasts were generally encased by stays and corsets. In the mid- to late nineteenth century, however, underbust corsets were introduced to grant more flexibility for popular recreational activities like tennis, golf and cycling, leaving the breasts unsupported.

Consequently, patents soon emerged for separate 'bust bodices' to address the emerging need for support and lift.[1] A brassiere-like 'breast pad' was registered as early as 1859[2], and a number of patents followed over subsequent decades, including one for a 'push-up' bodice patented in 1893.[3] The future of the bust bodice was firmly secured when the corset descended below the bust-line permanently, with the introduction of the S-bend corset in the very early 1900s. For a while, a low-slung bosom was fashionable – accentuated, even.[4] However, women with larger breasts still needed bust bodices, and then towards the end of the decade, the fashionable silhouette elongated and the bust bodice was worn more universally. The term brassiere was used in American *Vogue* in June 1907, and in English fashion magazines in the early 1910s. It seems to be an American appropriation of the Old French word for harness or shoulder strap.[5]

Several early twentieth-century designers claimed responsibility for popularizing the brassiere, including Madeleine Vionnet, Lucile and Paul Poiret, who said: '[It was] in the name of Liberty that I proclaimed the fall of the corset and the adoption of the brassiere.'[6] Certainly, by the end of the first decade, the brassiere was a must-have accessory, and throughout the twentieth century it was developed to lift, support and generally enhance the breasts – the 1920s being the only decade in which the breasts were deliberately flattened. The 1930s saw the general introduction of cup sizing, better elastics, and the adoption of the diminutive term 'bra'. It was also the decade in which women stopped wearing slips or petticoats underneath their bras, and started to wear them next to their skin. Innovation halted for the duration of the Second World War, but the 1950s saw the introduction of underwiring, padding, and stitching techniques that created an abstract conical shape. The 1960s and 1970s prized a more 'natural' look, mostly as a result of the youth revolution, but also in part because the women's rights movement politicized the bra and presented it as a symbol of chauvinism and oppression. For most women, however, the bra-less look was, ironically, often achieved with the help of a bra, and it remained an important part of the majority of women's wardrobes.

Today the bra represents the largest division of the underwear industry, accounting for the majority of its product development, profit and advertising. Modern bras are made from dozens of separate pieces, and utilize engineering principles and computer-generated stress data research in the search for perfect support and comfort.[7]

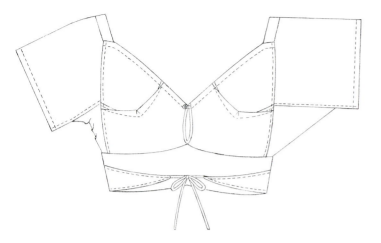
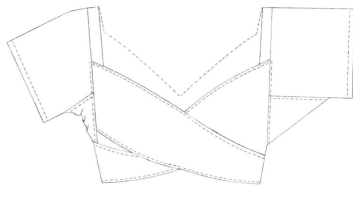

Most of the garments featured in this section date from the twentieth century. This cotton bust bodice, however, is a rare and notable exception, pre-dating most known garments of similar function and design by several decades or more.[8]

During the early part of the nineteenth century, the fashion was for neoclassical dresses with high underbust waistlines, skimming drapery, and often transparent fabrics (p.192). For the first time in centuries, breasts were not compressed by whalebone, but rather were fashionably defined, high and round, and for a period some women abandoned stays altogether.[9] Even so, some assistance was required to achieve the ideal figure. Fashion prints of the time show short waistcoats worn over dresses, and this bodice reveals that some form of improvised foundation garment was also worn underneath. It is home-made and fits quite a petite form. In the absence of stays, it offered a small measure of shaping – and some opacity under potentially transparent fabrics – without interfering with the fall of the dress.

It has a thick reinforcing band underneath the bosom, while a diamond-shaped gusset under each arm provides flexibility and fit. The centre-front fastens with a hand-made Dorset thread button – a wire ring worked around with cotton, much used through the eighteenth century but largely out of use by 1830. It shows signs of alteration at the shoulder seams and bust, where the original seaming has been darted to make the garment smaller. It is possible that it was worn by more than one woman over the years, or was altered by one after pregnancy and nursing.

The bodice shares similar characteristics with some bras of the early twentieth century, notably with its cross-over, wrap-around ties. This coincidence of function demonstrates the need for an adjustable grip around the ribcage, which was eventually perfected with the introduction of elastics towards the middle of the twentieth century.

Bust bodice
Britain, 1800–1830
Cotton, with Dorset thread button
V&A: T.341–1978

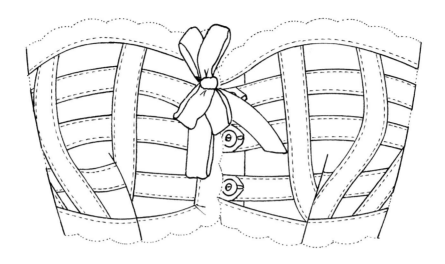

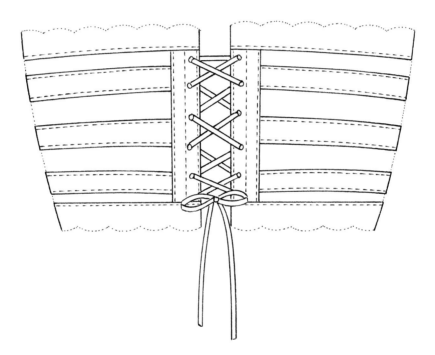

Around 1910, the voluptuous ideal of the preceding years was gradually replaced by a more slender silhouette as Parisian couturiers introduced a more elongated line. The puffed monobosom was still seen into the mid-1910s, but foundation garments were increasingly required to compress and smooth the figure. Bust bodices similar to this were advertised as 'bust confiners', designed to wear over the top of the corset to smooth the contours under the blouse or dress and to control and shape the bust, which was largely unsupported over the low, hip-confining corsets.[10]

This bust bodice is made of a lattice of figured silk ribbon, curving together at the bottom of the breast for shape and support. The ribbon sits on a ground of bobbin lace, which also trims the top and bottom. It was worn over both the chemise (or combinations, p.28) and the corset. It is probable that shoulder straps of figured silk were once attached to the bodice.

The bodice was sold at Dickins & Jones, then one of London's most famous department stores, with a reputation for selling high-quality drapery, linens and lingerie.[11]

Bust bodice
Dickins & Jones
Britain, 1910s
Figured silk satin ribbon and bobbin lace
V&A: T.33–1996

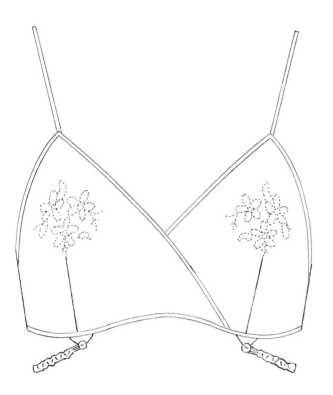
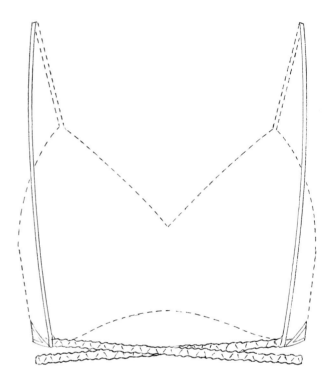

In 1926–7, Rosamond Klin[12], the director of London-based Kestos Ltd, began experimenting with new forms of brassiere. She began with two folded handkerchiefs, overlaid them, and attached shoulder straps. However, to achieve greater hold and support she attached long elastic ties to the back corner of the brassiere, wrapping them around the body and buttoning them securely under the cups. Whilst the design would not have offered much lift, it offered light compression and support without bulk, which perfectly complemented the sleek, bias-cut clothes of the 1930s. For the first time brassieres and girdles were worn without petticoats or slips underneath, to reduce bulges as much as possible.

Its simplicity of form meant that it was eminently affordable, and the design became so popular that women did not buy a brassiere, they bought a 'Kestos'. An advertisement from *Eve's Journal* magazine of November 1937 reads: 'On her entrance all heads turn, all male hearts miss a beat. She has not beauty in its truest sense, but elegance – and – what counts most of all, exquisiteness of form. Because she knows how much this means, Kestos has been her choice.'

This brassiere contains no label, but is identical to the Kestos design. It is made of silk with a small diamond of machine embroidery at the top of the cup. The back ties are made of a now very fragile rubber core under a ruched silk casing. The style was worn into the early 1950s, for day and eveningwear, and was even integrated into nightdresses and swimwear.

Brassiere
Kestos (or Kestos style)
Britain, 1930s
Silk, machine embroidery and elastic
Given by the family of Monica Maurice
V&A: T.789–1995

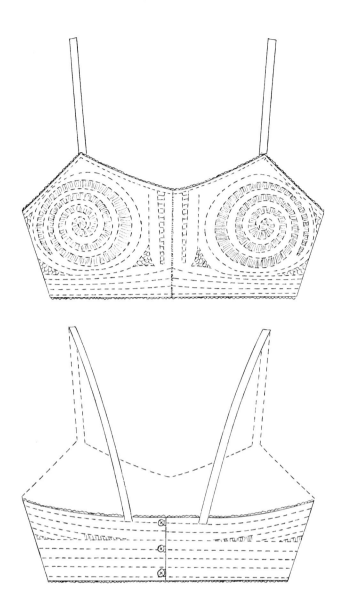

In the 1920s, women wore bandeau brassieres to flatten their breasts and create a straight boyish figure (p.100), however the brassiere of the 1930s separated and defined the breasts for a new sleek and gently curving figure. Along with the famous Kestos brand (p.148), another firm that capitalized on this change was J. Roussel of Paris, who had boutiques in Paris, London and across Britain.

J. Roussel was a popular brand from the early 1930s to the 1950s, selling corsets, panties, waspies, corselettes and brassieres. They were particularly famous for a type of brassiere unique to them, made from intricate knitted whirlpool patterns.[13] Introduced around 1928, its design created a softly rounded and defined shape. Finely knitted strips were laid in directional rows and spirals, some looping back on themselves in different directions, and interconnected with more loosely knitted inserts. The effect was not only decorative but offered elasticity via the pull and give of the knit; the tension in the closer knit strips provided support. The whirlpool technique was adapted in the 1950s and, employing sturdy fabrics, was used to create the fashionable conical breast shape of the decade.

Roussel's brassieres were advertised frequently in fashion magazines throughout the 1930s, as separate garments and as part of corselettes. It was still unusual for foundation garments to be without whalebone, and the advertisements proudly trumpeted its absence, stating that their knitted lace-style brassieres moulded to the body like a glove, were supple, light, and quick to put on and take off. They advised that since the effectiveness of the garment was entirely dependent upon the correct fit, their products were only sold at their own shops, where their trained saleswomen offered free fittings. There were several price ranges, dependent on whether the garment was ordered in cotton, cotton-silk mix or pure silk.[14] This brassiere would have been in the mid-range price.

Brassiere
J. Roussel of Paris
France (Paris) or Britain (London), 1930s
Silk and cotton, with silk satin ribbon
V&A: T.196–1989

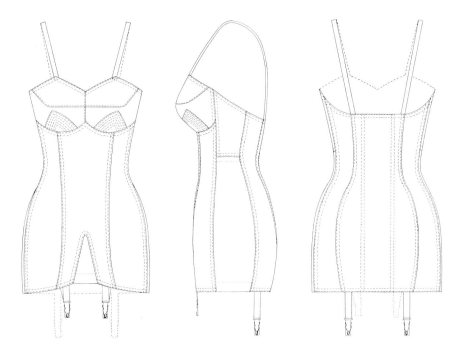

During the Second World War, materials were scarce and rationing was introduced to help control supply. The government slowed the production of foundationwear, as many of the materials used for corsets were also particularly required for the war effort. However, an article in *The Times* of 23 November 1940, stated that 95 per cent of women did not consider corsets a luxury and that working women especially depended upon them for 'support and comfort'.

This corselette was made by Leethams of Portsmouth, under the brand name Twilfit, as part of the British Civilian Clothing Act or 'Utility Scheme', enforced from June 1942. The act restricted the use of certain fabrics and forbade unnecessary decorative trimmings. This corselette supports the breast with a simple triangular panel at the underside of the breast, which is shaped and reinforced with stitching.

Utility corselette
Leethams (Twilfit) Ltd
Britain (Portsmouth), 1940s
Rayon satin and elastic, coutille, and steel boning
Given by Mr Ian Chipperfield
V&A: T.175–1998

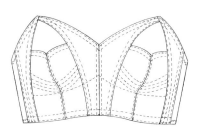 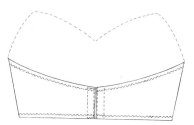

The bra shown here is an example of a 'cathedral' bra, popular in the 1950s and so-called because when the bra is worn the bones create pointed arches over the breasts. The bones also separate and define the breasts, pressing them from the sides into the pointed, or bullet, shape fashionable during the 1950s.

The bra was designed to be worn with strapless cocktail dresses and evening gowns. However, the couturiers that popularized the strapless look did so with specially constructed corsets built into the bodices of their dresses, which made them very secure. The cathedral bra, on the other hand, was likely to slip down or need adjustment throughout the evening, and consequently the market for them was relatively short lived.

'Cathedral' bra
Au Fait Foundations
Britain, 1953
Rayon satin and elastic, coutille, and steel boning
V&A: T.104–1981

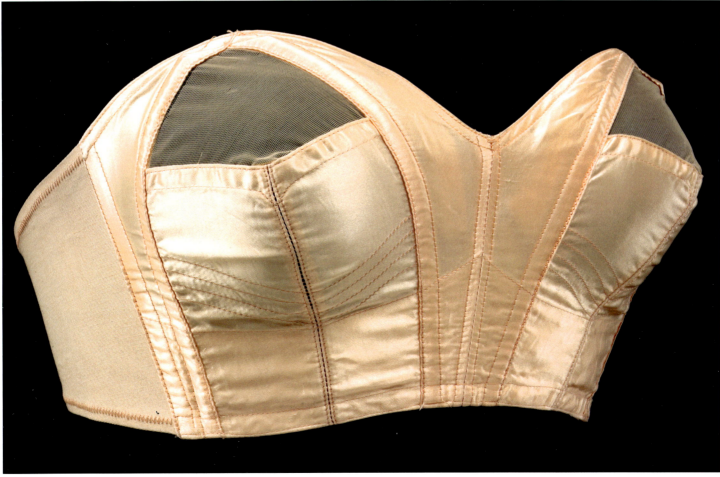

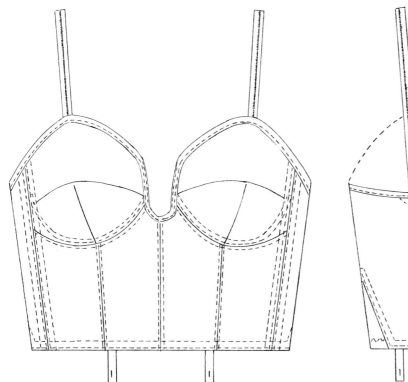
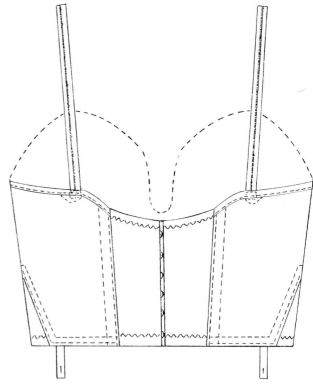

Metal attachments for bust bodices and brassieres are recorded in patents and advertisements from the late nineteenth century onwards, but underwired cups as we know them were introduced in the 1930s. In 1931, Helene Pons – on behalf of the Van Raalte Company of New York – was granted a patent for an 'open-ended wire loop' that curved around the underside of each breast.[15] This was followed over subsequent years by similar patents, using wire to 'separate' or 'support' the breasts.[16]

Underwired bras started to appear on the market in numbers towards the end of the decade, but the Second World War stalled these developments for most of the 1940s because steel was commandeered for the war effort and its supply strictly controlled. However, underwire re-entered the market and grew in popularity throughout the 1950s, when it helped to provide the uplift and definition needed to create the fashionably high, pert bosom.

This long-line bra was made by Rigby & Peller in the 1950s. The company was established in 1939 by Bertha Rigby and Gita Peller in South Molton Street, London, and taken over by Peller's cousin, Mrs Seiden, in the mid-1950s. Rigby & Peller specialized in bespoke, high-end corsetry and lingerie, and was granted the Royal Warrant as corsetier to the Queen in 1960.

This bra is made with nylon, elasticized nylon netting, and steel underwires – all of which were, at that time, exciting, modern features. It is called a 'divorce' bra because the cups separate the breasts. The skin is protected from the underwiring by thick plush, while the four elastic tabs at the bottom of the bra allow it to be buttoned securely onto a girdle. For more on Rigby and Peller see p.210.

'Divorce' bra
Rigby & Peller
Britain (London), 1950s
Nylon, elastic and steel
Given by Rigby & Peller
V&A: T.634–1995

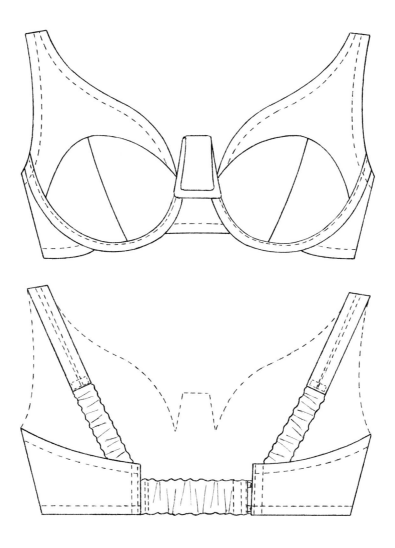

In the late 1950s, improvements in dyeing techniques allowed for affordable commercial use of stable bright colours. Coinciding with the teen revolution of the early 1960s, these colours were applied in playful, bold and youthful patterns on all types of underwear.

This bra illustrates the development from the conical and pointed look of the 1950s, to the softer, rounded shape and construction style that became standard in the 1960s and is used to the present day. The cups are padded with wadding to give fullness and a smooth line. They are pieced with a horizontal seam across the middle of the bosom, and a vertical seam at the underside, providing both roundness and uplift. The directionally laid pieces provide shaping, while the seams reinforce the fabric and stop it from stretching. This technique is called 'cut and sew'. Bras of the 1950s were largely made with horizontal seams only, or with circular stitching, to create the exaggerated 'bullet' shape. There is no stretch in the fabric of this bra, and the cup continues up in one piece to the shoulder strap. There is an elastic strip at the back, covered with matching ruched fabric, to allow for stretch and a snug fit around the ribs.

The curvaceous, push-up effect of this bra contrasted with the concurrent androgyny of the decade. More Brigitte Bardot than Twiggy, this bra demonstrates the multiplicity of fashionable images and ideals present in the 1960s. In a major shift from the 1950s, both voluptuous and skinny figures were expected to be so naturally, without the aid of girdles or corsetry. The fashionable body was young and firm, and wearing foundation garments was increasingly seen as a sign of old age or physical weakness. Girdles were still sold, but they were not featured in fashion magazines or advertised quite as proudly as they once were. Matching bra and knickers sets were established as the dominant fashion in underwear, and remain so today.

Bra
Britain, 1960s
Printed cotton, underwiring, and foam
Given by Caroline Wren
V&A: T.142–2000

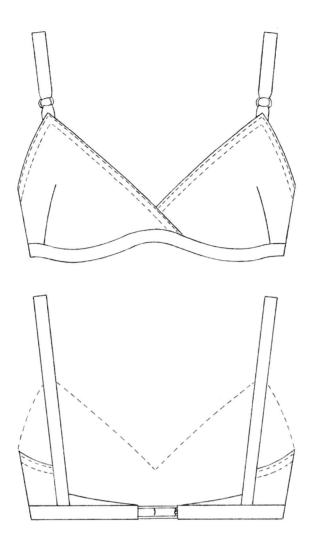

In the 1960s it became fashionable to have an adolescent, skinny body, as personified by models like Twiggy. Control garments were seen as a sign of age or infirmity, and underwear was streamlined and reduced. Stockings and suspenders gave way to tights, and girdles to Lycra panties, while the truly fashionable figure required no support at all.

Towards the mid-1960s, fashion designers were experimenting with new fabrics and structures that abstracted the body and broke with existing fashions. Not only was the miniskirt introduced, but designers such as Paco Rabanne and André Courrèges presented collections made from interlocking metal discs and transparent plastics that revealed the body underneath. In 1964, the California-based fashion designer Rudi Gernreich introduced the transparent chiffon see-through blouse, and the topless bikini – essentially bikini bottoms with narrow braces. His designs were written off by many as publicity stunts; others were outraged and picketed shops that sold them.[17] Gernreich's notoriety was a good marketing tool, and in the same year the American lingerie company Exquisite Form commissioned him to design a bra, known as the 'no bra' bra. A card included with the bra featured a picture of Gernreich, along with the following background information: 'The revolutionary designer of the topless bathing suit and see-through evening blouse is famous for the natural bare look even in his covered up fashions. That's why it's news when he, of all designers, designs a bra. No gimmick, the "NO BRA" bra supports yet gives you the natural nude look of a firm, young, bra-less bosom.' The bra was a success, and prompted a wave of imitators. As *Time* magazine of March 1965 reports: 'Items like Rudi Gernreich's no-bra bra and Warner's body stockings have proved pacesetters for a rash of stretchable flesh-colored garments that look like a second skin.'

The bra is made of two transparent nylon triangles that meet with a slight overlap at the centre-front and extend round to the hook-and-eye back fastening. The cups are shaped with a single diagonal dart. It is very lightweight, offering little lift, and would have been worn by women who needed minimal or no support, but who were perhaps too accustomed to wearing bras to go without.

'No bra' bra
Rudy Gernreich (1922–85), for Exquisite Form
USA, 1964
Nylon
V&A:T.35–1999

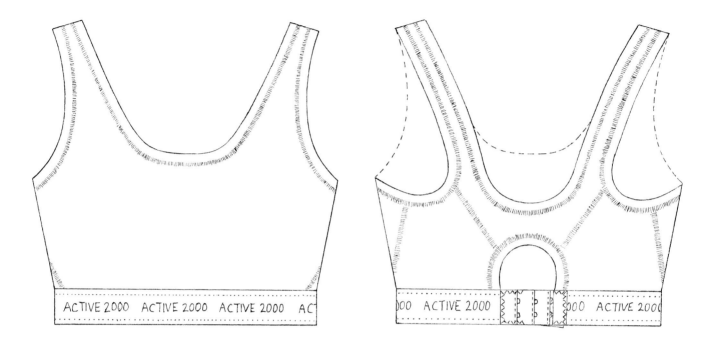

From the 1970s onwards, exercise became the fashionable method of figure control. The favoured body was slim but toned, and Jane Fonda and other leotard-clad fitness gurus led record numbers of women in aerobics and exercise classes. In 1977, American designers and jogging partners, Hinda Miller and Lisa Lindahl, created a jogging bra made from two jock-straps, to stop women's breasts bouncing as they exercised. At first, sports bras worked by compressing the breasts, but developments in synthetic stretch fabrics soon allowed for sophisticated supporting and breathable garments.[18]

This sports bra is made from an elasticized nylon material called Tactel, introduced in 1983. It is well suited to exercise, being durable, breathable and quick drying. It has a soft cotton-like finish but is so highly tensile that it requires no seaming to provide the appropriate support and hold. The material stretches to fit the body, but returns to its original shape when taken off.

This bra was made by Marks & Spencer in 1996. Marks & Spencer was founded in 1884 and is one of the most established clothing and homeware stores on the British high street. It is also one of the most important names in the history of underwear. In 1988, *The Daily Telegraph* dubbed the company 'the guardians of the nation's nether regions'. In 1996 – the year this bra was made – M&S held 35 per cent of the British underwear market.[19] They first started selling hosiery and lingerie items in the 1920s and were at the forefront of developing and using synthetic fibres to make quality, affordable underwear. The company has always invested in scientific and technological research: they were among the very first to offer rayon in the 1930s, and nylon underwear in the late 1940s. They were also ahead of the game in incorporating Lycra into their products. Lycra became popular in the 1980s, but was used in M&S's 'Waistline Bras' as early as 1970.[20]

Sports bra
Marks & Spencer
Britain, 1996
Tactel nylon with cotton
V&A: T.498–1996

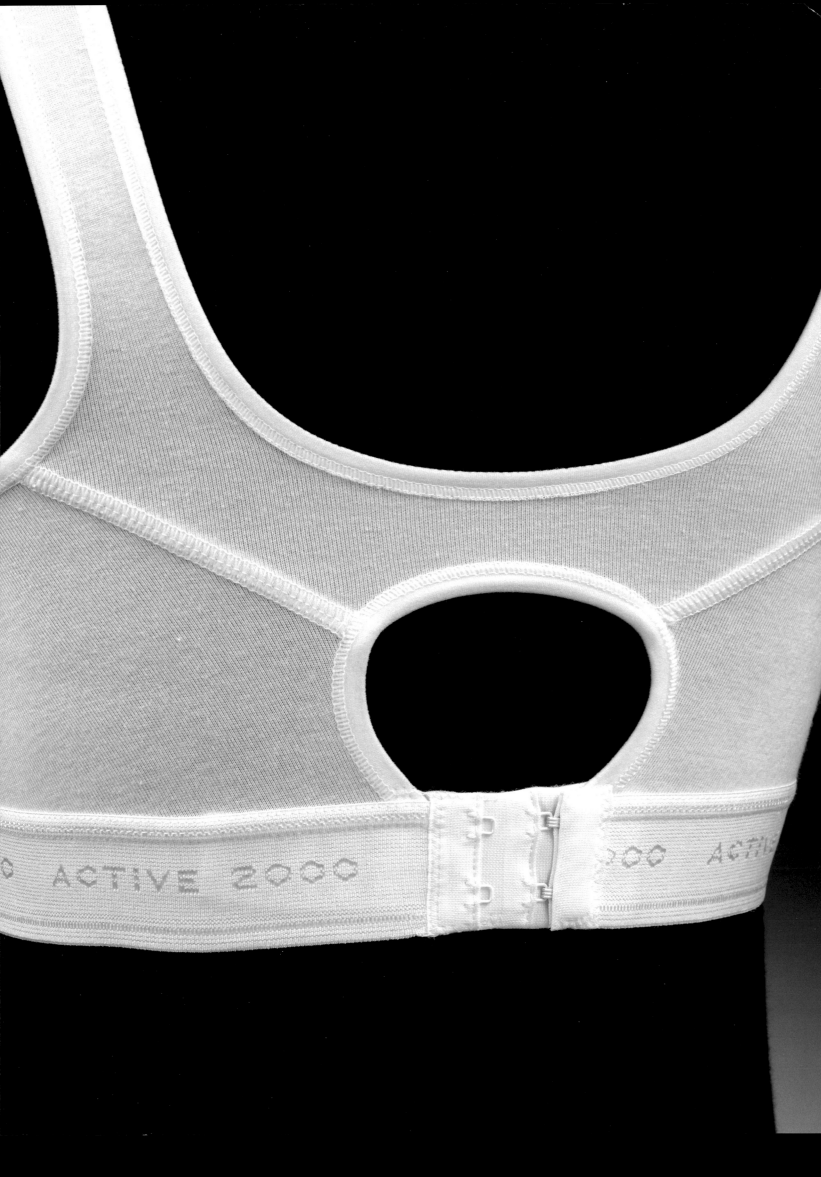

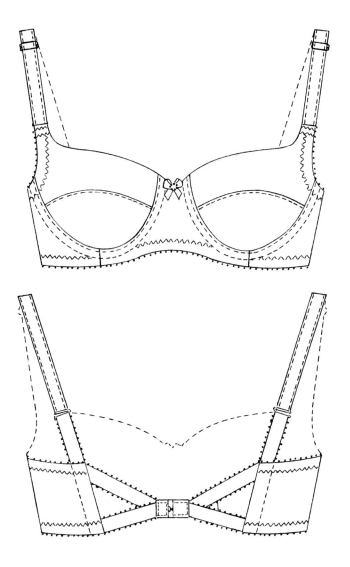

Gossard launched the Ultrabra plunge bra in 1994, with the advertising tagline: 'Ultrabra, creating the ultimate cleavage'. It was followed by additions to the range, including 'Ultrabra Perfection', 'Ultrabra Light' and the 'Ultrabra Super Boost', which launched in 1999 with the slogan: 'Biggest Cleavage EVER . . . Or your money back!'

Ultrabra's primary product is the plunge bra – a low-cut bra whose cups are joined at the centre-front by only a narrow connecting tab. The plunge bra creates cleavage through a combination of diagonal seaming and padded cups. The seam is cut at a high diagonal angle, and causes the sparingly cut underpiece to push the breasts together from the sides. The version shown here is a balcony bra, and is made slightly differently. The seaming is on a lower diagonal and is heavily padded at the underside of the cup. This pushes the breasts upwards and creates a high, rounded and defined cleavage, but with more separation between the breasts. The bra is made of glossy, satin-finish nylon, and has pockets at the interior underside of the cup, into which optional pads can be inserted for maximum lift and cleavage.

Gossard was founded in Chicago by Henry Williamson Gossard in 1901. In 1921, the company opened a shop in Regent Street, London, and in 1926 a Gossard factory was opened in Leighton Buzzard, Bedfordshire. In the 1930s Gossard ceased to be an American company and became a British public company instead. For many years they held the license to make the Wonderbra, whose patent is owned by a Canadian lingerie company called Canadelle Ltd. Gossard introduced the Wonderbra to the British market in 1969, but lost the license to manufacture the brand to Canadelle's sister company Playtex in 1994. At the time Gossard lost the license, the Wonderbra accounted for 12 per cent of the British bra market. The Ultrabra was launched as a competitor to the Wonderbra, and began what was known as the 'Bra Wars', as the two firms fought for dominance of the massively profitable industry with high profile print and billboard advertisements.[21]

'Ultrabra Perfection' balcony bra
Gossard
Britain, 1997
Nylon, polyester and elastane, with underwiring
V&A: T.500–1997

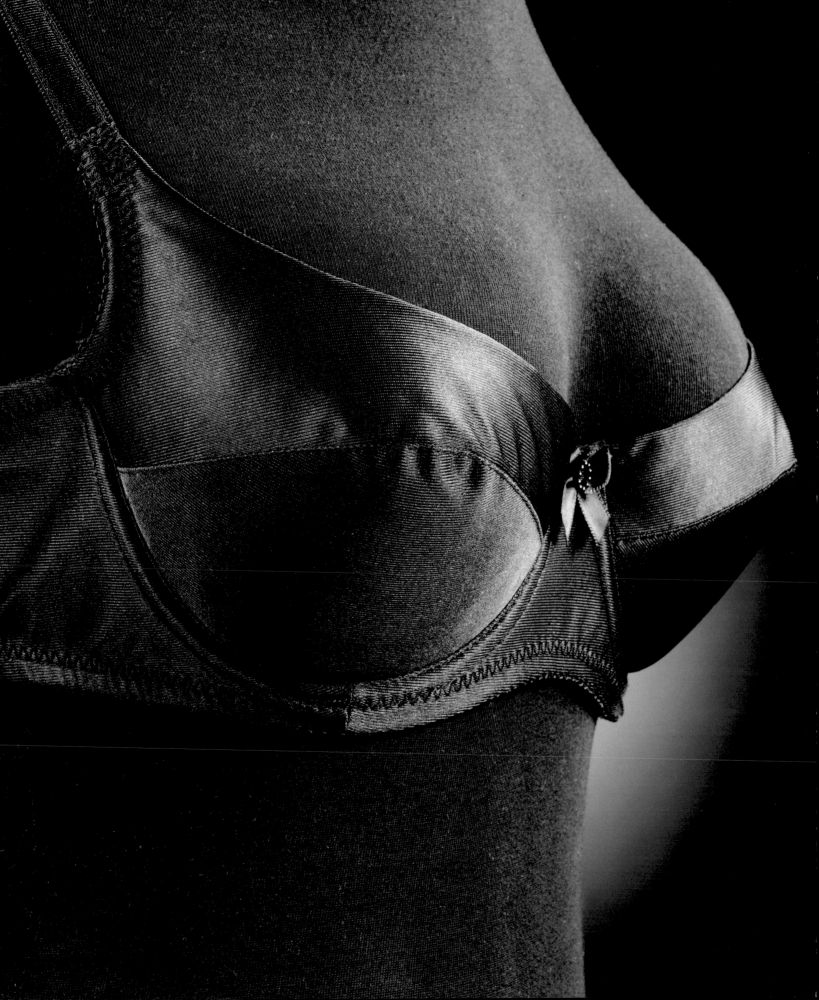

VOLUME

*Numberless are the devices made use of by the people of fashion
to avoid the pursuit of the vulgar . . . Of all the articles . . . the hoop hath stood
the longest . . . it being found impossible to convey seven yards of hoop
into a hackney-coach, or to slide with it behind a counter.*

Henry Fielding, 1752[1]

Just as the waist has been reduced and shaped throughout the centuries, so have other parts of the body been artificially padded and bolstered into stylized angles and curves. The hips and buttocks have often been exaggerated by undergarments such as hoops, bustles and crinolines, and the upper body has been augmented with pads, ruffles and boning, to accentuate the curve of the breasts.

Volume in dress began as a demonstration of status, providing wide foundations for the conspicuous display of costly fabrics and trimmings, and demonstrating that the wearer lived a life of fashionable leisure – her very clothes rendering her incapable of practical work. The earliest object included in this chapter is a side hoop from 1778. Side hoops were wide petticoats that gave the skirt an abstracted square shape, and were fashionable for a large part of the eighteenth century. They were made with cane or whalebone strips threaded into horizontal casings along the petticoat, and pulled inwards from the front and back with internal tapes. The hoops protruded horizontally from the hip and were the subject of many satirical and moralizing pamphlets, due to their propensity to take up space and the risk they posed of accidental exposure if the wind blew them up. Such extreme foundations were not new to fashion. In the fifteenth and sixteenth centuries, the farthingale petticoat was the height of fashionable dress. Farthingales were exaggerated bell- or barrel-shaped petticoats, made from hoops of cane or whalebone sewn onto stiff fabrics like buckram in horizontal rows.

The majority of objects included in this chapter are from the nineteenth century, when skirts saw their greatest number of fluctuations in shape. At the beginning of the century, fashionable dresses were briefly tubular, but skirts began to widen again during the 1810s, and by the 1830s the figure was inflated with a bell-shaped skirt and extravagantly padded balloon sleeves. The skirt reached an extreme circumference in the 1850s, and industrial developments intervened to lighten the load with a cage crinoline that reduced the weight and number of petticoats needed. The cage crinoline was made of horizontal hoops of spring steel attached to strips of fabric. Spring steel was light and flexible, and was capable of returning to its original shape if sat on or crushed. When the crinoline subsided in the 1860s, the volume moved to the back and was supported by flat-fronted crinolettes (half-crinolines), and by bustle pads and wire frames. At its most extreme, during the mid- to late 1880s, the bustle jutted out horizontally from the small of the back, causing cartoonists to draw women with tea-trays resting on their derrières.[2] From the late 1890s, the skirt gradually became more fitted around the hip, and remained relatively modest until the end of the 1930s, when Parisian couturiers briefly revived crinoline and bustle shapes – foreshadowing Christian Dior's post-war 'New Look' of 1947, with its padded hips, full skirts, and exaggerated feminine curves.

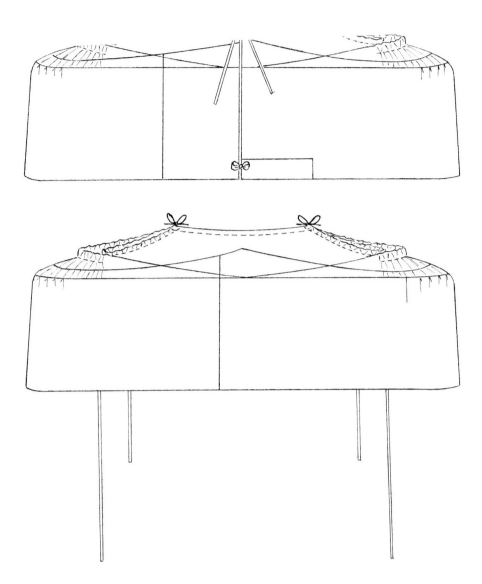

For most of the eighteenth century, hooped petticoats dominated women's dress. They first appeared around 1710 and were fairly small and rather cone-shaped, though by the 1740s they were vast ovals that protruded sharply out to the sides.

In 1745, a pamphlet was published called *The Enormous Abomination of the Hoop Petticoat as the Fashion now is*, which condemned the hoop as a public nuisance. The writer said that the massive hoops took up too much space on pavements and in carriages, and that by lifting them up to step through mud in the street the wearer caused her ankles and lower legs to be disgracefully visible. In addition – as women did not take to wearing drawers until the following century – newspapers and magazines often featured articles complaining that a sudden movement, a gust of wind, or a fall, resulted in embarrassing exposure.[3] One writer to *The London Magazine* in 1741 hoped to influence women against the wearing of hoops by persuading them that it was unattractive: 'I know no other Argument should sooner prevail with them, than to acquaint them it is a Mode very disagreeable to the Men in general.'[4] However the wearing of hoops was arguably not about attractiveness at all, but about the demonstration of status and gentility, for the hoop supported massive skirts that were designed to demonstrate the wearer's wealth – or rather that of her family – by the conspicuous amount of fine embroidery and costly fabric that she wore.

This side hoop is very rare, as it was given to the Museum complete with its original receipt, recording the sale of a gown and 'pink Holland hoop'[5] to one Miss David for ten shillings and six pence on 16 February 1778. The merchant was Andrew Shabner, a robe-maker at 26 Tavistock Street, Covent Garden.

Side hoop
Andrew Shabner (dates unknown)
Britain (London), 1778
Linen and cane
From the family of Mrs Deborah Carter, given by Mr and Mrs R.C. Carter
V&A: T.120–1969

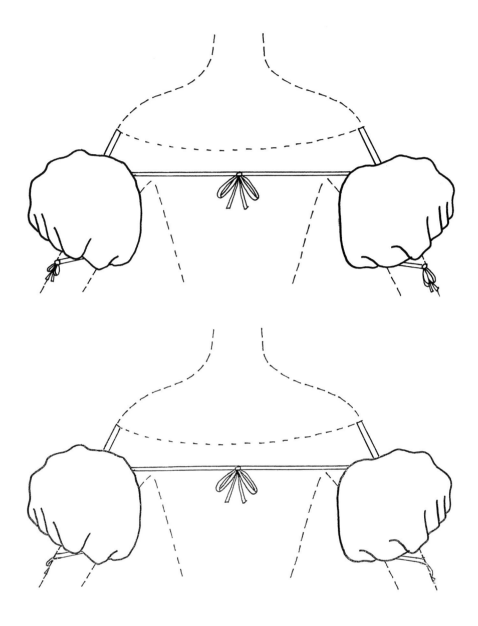

By the mid-1820s, fashion was moving away from the tubular classicism of the Regency period. The waist was descending from its 1815 high point under the bust, and was moving towards its natural level, which began once again to be defined and shaped. Fuller skirts and ballooning sleeves contributed to this new curvaceousness, creating a figure of inflated proportions. The fashionable sleeve style – known as a leg of mutton, or gigot sleeve – was tight at the lower arm but puffed outwards from the elbow around the upper arm.

These cotton sleeve pads are filled with down and were worn around the upper arm to support and fill the voluminous sleeve. The idea was not to create a puffed, high shoulder, but to continue and exaggerate a sloping downwards line. Some supports were built into the sleeve, but others such as these were separate accessories. They could be reinforced with cane or wire, or made of stiff fabrics like buckram. Pads like these, made of feathers, could be manipulated and adjusted more easily than stiffer types.

These sleeve pads were held in place with tapes (now cut off) that were tacked onto the corset.

Sleeve pads
Britain, 1820s or 1830s
Cotton and down
Gift of Miss Frances E. White
V&A: T.189D&C–1921

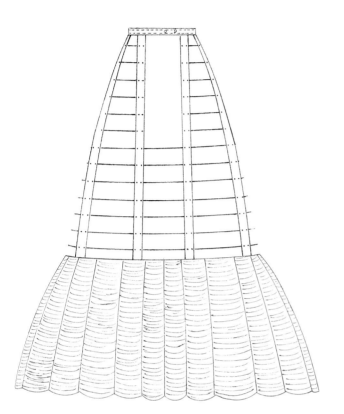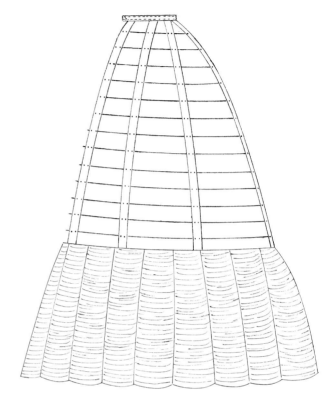

Throughout the 1840s and 1850s, the fashionable skirt expanded and women had to wear an average of four to six petticoats to achieve the desired dome shape. In addition to various layers of muslin and flannel, stiff crinoline petticoats were worn. The crinoline was named after the French word for horsehair (*'crin'*), which was woven into the petticoat along with a warp of cotton or wool. By the early 1850s, even horsehair was insufficient to carry the enormous weight of the many layers, and dressmakers began inserting whalebone into the structure of their dresses and reinforcing fabrics with cording.

In July 1856, the first British patent for the cage crinoline was registered by one C. Amet on behalf of French inventor R.C. Milliet of Besançon.[6] The patent was for a 'skeleton petticoat made of steel springs fastened to tape'.[7] Competing inventors and manufacturers presented interpretations of the design, and the cage crinoline was soon big business, helped in no small measure by the couturier Charles Frederick Worth, who incorporated the steel cage into designs for his influential client, the Empress Eugénie. The *Englishwoman's Domestic Magazine*, like many other publications, disseminated information about the Empress's tastes, reporting in June 1861 that to support a simple day dress, she wore a 'moderate sized steel petticoat, and a muslin one – with, of course, a plain one over it'.

This cage crinoline is made from hoops of spring steel, a resilient metal which keeps its shape despite bending or twisting. The hoops are fixed onto tapes with stamped metal eyelets, and the waistband is made of wool. The bulk of the cage is mostly at the back, as by the mid-1860s the dome-shaped skirt of the late 1850s had flattened slightly at the front. A deep flounce of thick cotton woven with horsehair encircles the hem.

The invention of the cage crinoline was a catalyst for the widespread adoption of drawers, as the wind was liable to blow the buoyant cage up, suddenly revealing all. A visitor to England records their bouncy movement: '[Women] walk along rustling, their dress follows and precedes them like the ticking of a clock . . . Energetic, discordant, jerking.'[8]

Cage crinoline
Britain, *c.*1867
Spring steel, with horsehair and cotton, metal eyelets and woollen waistband
Given by Mr F.D. Worthington
V&A: Circ.87–1951

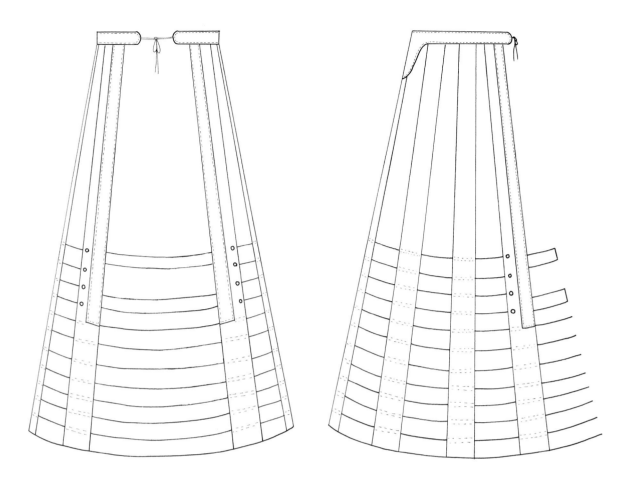

The introduction of the cage crinoline in the 1850s heralded a new era of mass-production in the clothing industry. Wearing large crinoline skirts began as an upper-class fashion, but spring steel cage crinolines were easily machine-made using few materials, making them quick and cheap to produce. Women from all classes were able to purchase and wear them, even to work, and newspapers reported stories of workers in porcelain and glass factories knocking stock from the shelves with sweeps of their enormous cages; a frequent 1860s complaint was that even maids were wearing them in emulation of their mistresses.[9]

The largest and most well-known manufacturer of cage crinolines was the American firm of W.S. & E.H. Thomson, with branches in England, France and Germany, in addition to the United States. The London factory, established in the East End in 1862, employed 1,000 workers and produced about 4,000 crinolines a day, and the number of hooks and eyes used equated to nearly a quarter of a million. In twelve years the German factory alone manufactured almost ten million crinolines. Thomson's also introduced a corset and bustle line.[10]

Thomson's 'Crown' crinolines were the most popular brand of the 1860s, and were generally considered superior to others.

The English Woman's Domestic Magazine of October 1862 wrote: 'To those ladies who prefer . . . cages, we recommend Thomson's patent crown skirts, as being very durable, and not easily bent or broken. The steels are threaded on very broad strong binding, each steel being secured by a metal eyelet-hole, so well fastened that it is impossible for it to slip . . . We know Thomson's skirts to be very strong and durable, but would recommend any of our readers who think of purchasing one to have it covered inside and out, to the height of about eighteen inches, with some material, either white or coloured, to prevent any accident occurring by the foot catching in the steel.'[11]

This crinoline is from the 'Empress' line, whose name invoked the very fashionable and much-emulated crinoline wearer, the Empress Eugénie. It is made of vertical wool braid bands, through which are threaded the covered spring steel hoops. There are eight steel hoops that encircle the wearer from the hem up, and four additional half-hoops surrounding the back and sides but not the front panel, so as to allow the wearer some comfort and practicality when walking and sitting down. Magazines frequently presented crinoline skirts of massive proportions, but this modest practical crinoline demonstrates that not all were executed to fashion plate ideals.

'Empress' cage crinoline
W.S. & E.H. Thomson
Britain (London), 1865–8
Spring steel and wool braid, with cotton waistband
Bequeathed by Mr E.W. Mynott
V&A: T.51–1980

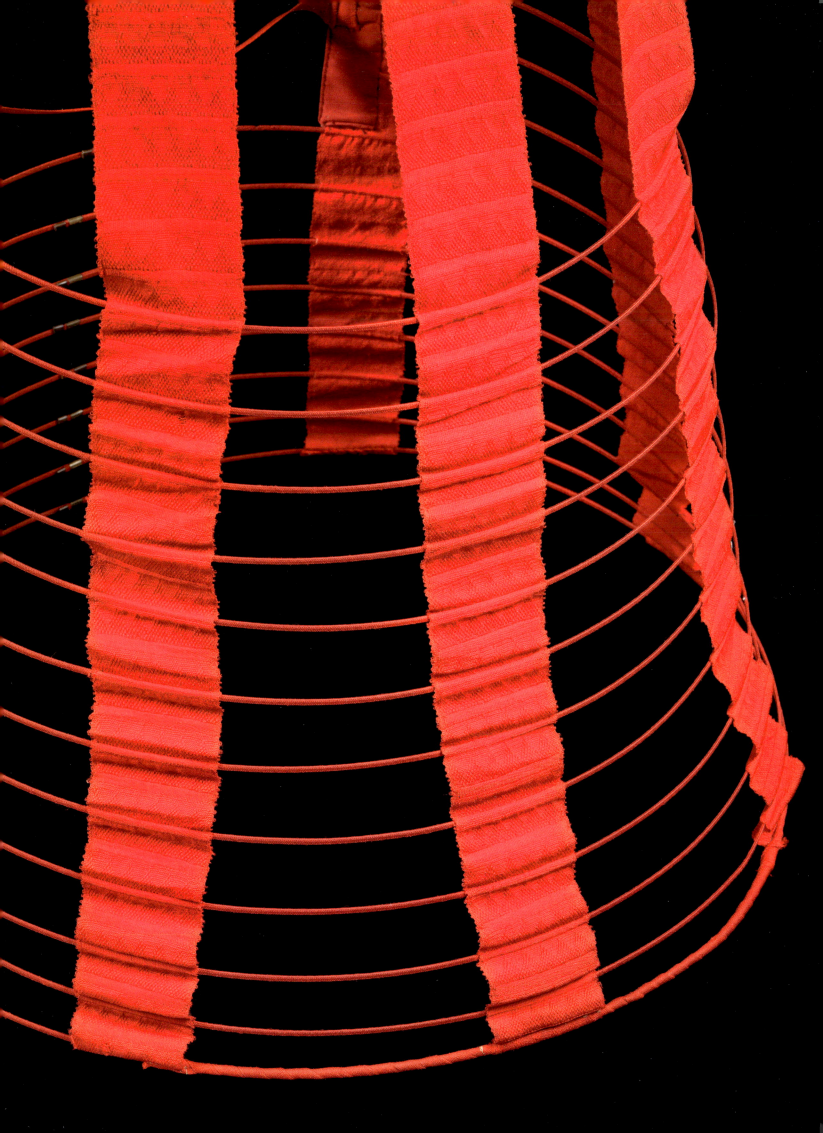

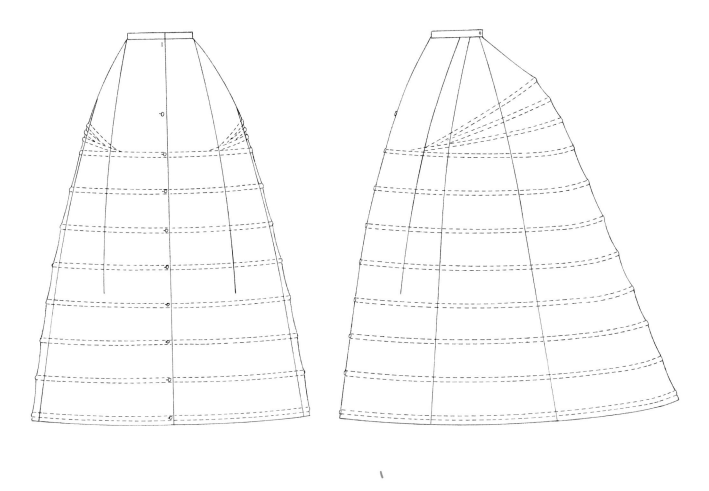

As the 1860s progressed, the voluminous crinoline skirt was abandoned by the upper classes, partly because cage crinolines were so affordable that they were being worn by the lower classes, and also because they were so inconvenient. They were difficult to manoeuvre up stairs and through doorways, and were so large in some instances that carriages and seats had to be reconfigured to accommodate them. Some cages were fitted with hinges and springs so that they could be concertinaed up or in as required, but stories persisted in magazines and newspapers of crinolines getting caught under wheels, drifting into lit fireplaces, or being blown up by the wind.[12]

So by the middle of the 1860s there was a distinct flattening of skirt fronts, and the fashionable shape was shifting its weight backwards. The surplus fabric of the formerly vast skirts was draped up and eventually supported and padded out further by bustles. This crinoline marks the mid-point between the crinoline and the bustle, showing the evolution of fashion from one trend to the next.

The crinoline shown here is made of cane hoops covered completely with white cotton. The canes sit in hand-stitched horizontal channels, with openings that allow them to be removed for washing. The cotton gathers neatly at the waistband and fastens at the front with buttons.

Crinoline
Britain, 1860s
Cane and cotton
V&A: T.16–1979

When the crinoline started to subside towards the end of the 1860s, dresses became more moulded to the torso. The volume of the skirts shifted towards the back into gathered drapes and folds, supported by a crinolette or half-crinoline. This crinolette features a number of internal tapes so that the bustle shape can be pulled in, heightened, or widened to complement different dresses. Around 1870, the bustle was positioned at the small of the back, but in following years it was worn lower down, towards the base of the spine.

Crinolette
Britain, *c.*1870
Spring steel and cotton with braid edging
Given by Messrs Harrods Ltd
V&A: T.775C–1913

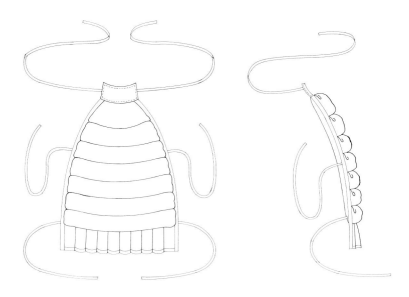

By the mid-1870s the skirt had narrowed still further, with the emphasis on the bustle, train and drapery at the back. The fashionable bodice – known as the 'cuirass' bodice – was elongated with a seamless waist ending at, or below, the hips. The bustle pad was lengthened and worn low to continue the body's fluid and gently curving line. This bustle is made from rows of padded horsehair rolls, machine-stitched onto a horsehair ground and gathered into a frill at the bottom. It is covered with horsehair and linen, woven into a pattern of vertical stripes alternating with bands of checks, and edged with striped cotton tape.

Bustle pad
Britain, *c.*1875
Woven horsehair and linen, padded with horsehair
Bequeathed by Mr E.W. Mynott
V&A: T.57–1980

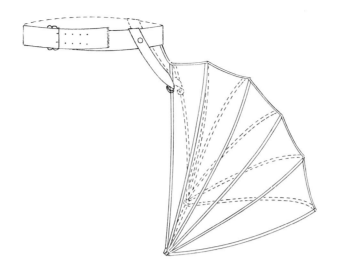

Stapley & Smith were manufacturers of foundation garments, based in East London. They advertised widely in the 1870s and 1880s, and were among the first companies to register their underwear designs.[13] The print on the adjustable waist tape of this bustle reads: 'The New Phantom. Beware of spurious imitations. See that every bustle bears the Trade Mark "Phantom". Regd. No. 72855 Patent Applied for. S&S London'. No patent was granted, but the number sequence relates to applications for 1884.[14]

This bustle was arranged so that it folded up when the wearer sat down and was considered a great technological innovation. Six curved steel wires are looped at each end around one main straight axis, which allows them to pivot up and down.

'The New Phantom' bustle frame
Stapley & Smith
Britain (London), 1884–5
Steel and cotton twill tape, with stamped metal eyelets and metal buckle
Given by Miss Mary Montefiore
V&A:T.131C–1919

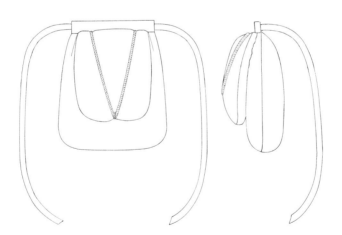

By 1880 the bustle had all but disappeared, making a re-emergence around 1883. However, instead of the low drapery of the mid-to late 1870s, the new style was sharp and angular, jutting out at right angles to the body. This square bustle pad is made from glazed calico trimmed with silk cord, and fastened with a waist tape. It is stuffed to a very solid shape with straw and would have been worn with several petticoats. A faded paper label with blue print writing is stuck to the waist tape and reads 'Au Louvre Paris', the name of a grand Parisian department store that opened around the middle of the century.

Bustle pad
France (Paris), c.1885
Glazed calico stuffed with straw
V&A:T.337–1978

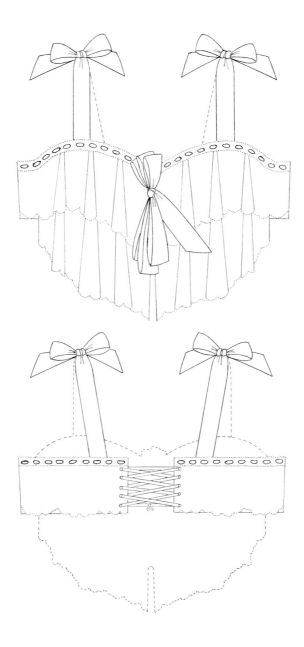

The S-bend corset was introduced in the first years of the twentieth century (p.96). It was cut lower than those of the 1890s, to free the diaphragm in the name of health. This left the bosom unsupported, and the low-slung, buxom shape that resulted became highly fashionable, and was soon exaggerated and promoted by fashion magazines. To achieve the new ideal shape, some women required assistance from foundation garments. *The Lady's Realm* of March 1901 stated: 'The new cut of corset, of course, drops the bust, and to attain that curved look so essential to a good figure it is necessary for thin women to have a ruching or even two ruchings of ribbon put inside the new, low-busted corset.'

'Bust improvers' had been advertised since the middle of the nineteenth century. They were generally padded inserts or canvas-covered wire cups that were tucked into the tops of corsets, though pills and creams also claimed to more permanently enhance the bosom.[15] During the reign of the S-bend, however, bust improvers became wholly separate from the corset.

This bust improver is made of silk satin faced with layers of lace. The lace overhangs the satin band to add blousing and volume at the bodice, which was then captured in at a slender waist. Three vertical whalebone strips are stitched into casings in each cup to provide structure and shape, and are overlaid with a layer of silk plush for comfort. The bodice laces at the back, with thick silk satin ribbon shoulder straps and a decorative bow over three front-fastening buttons. It would have been worn over a chemise or combinations.

Bust bodice
France, *c*.1905
Silk satin, machine lace and silk satin ribbon, with whalebone, silk plush and metal eyelets
T.340–1978

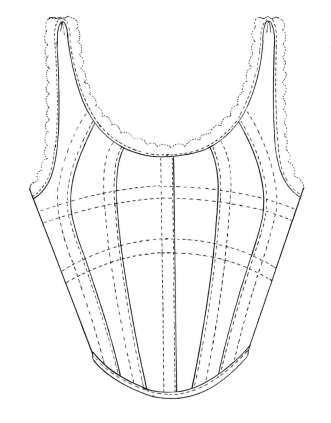

The bodice shown here is described as a 'bust extender, style 50' in a 1913 Spirella mail-order catalogue. It states that 'because of its boning and contour [the bust extender] gives natural lines to the person who is too thin or scant in chest development'. It goes on: 'Spirella bust extenders are designed for slender to medium figures with bust and chest development small in proportion to waist size and shoulder breadth. Style 50 is intended for the slender, long waisted figure.' It promises that as a result of the curved bones, it is self-supporting and requires no padding, and is made of 'light, strong, white batiste, daintily trimmed with lace . . . Beautifully curved to produce roundness in front of under arm where slender figure is usually deficient, as well as in the bust'. The company also offered bust confiners for women with 'overdeveloped' bosoms.[16]

The unboned cotton batiste of the back section tapers into narrow ties that wrap around the body and tie in front. It was worn over a corset and a chemise, along with drawers and several layers of petticoats. A looped tape at the bottom centre-front of the bodice, called a 'stay hook', secured the bodice to the corset. An interior label reads: 'Spirella Corsets, Trademark Unbreakable'.

The Spirella Corset Company was established in Letchworth, Hertfordshire, in May 1910, following the development of spiral steel bones by Marcus Merritt Beeman in 1904, and the consequent foundation of the Spirella Company in Pennsylvania, USA.[17] The company also had factories and offices in Canada, Sweden and Germany.

Bust bodice
Spirella Corsets
Britain (Letchworth), 1910–4
Cotton batiste trimmed with machine lace trim, with spiral steel boning
Jean Muir collection
V&A: T.348–1996

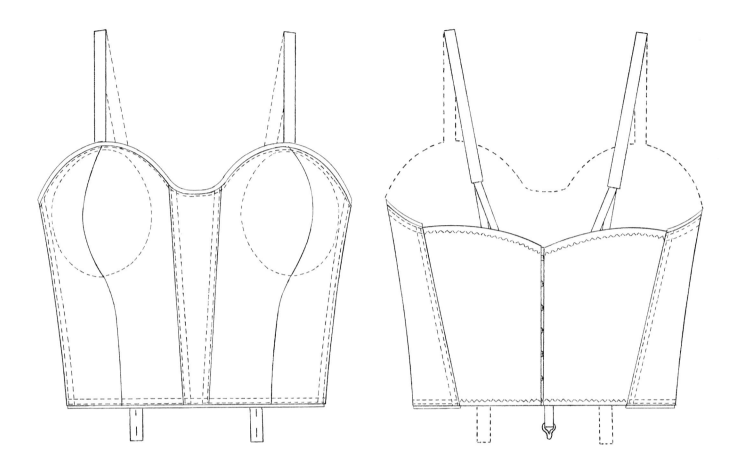

Madame Illa Knina was a famous Mayfair corsetiere with prestigious clients that included royalty and Hollywood actresses. She played on her exclusive image to advertise her ready-to-wear and mail-order ranges as 'the haute couture of corsetry'.[18] She also had mass-market ambitions and designed several ranges for Marks and Spencer. She used new fabrics such as nylons and innovative printing techniques and dyes, creating bold and colourful patterns that appealed to the emerging youth market.

This three-quarter-length bra is made of a plain nylon. At the bottom are elastic tabs to secure it to a matching girdle and to pull it taut. It is lightly boned with spiral steels at the centre-front to separate the breasts. Some of the seams and the shoulder straps are lined with nylon velveteen. The garment is rather simple, creating a plain, sleek foundation for its signature feature: solid foam rubber cones, stitched into each cup.

The 1950s trend for pointed breasts meant that a large percentage of bras were shaped with artificial cups like this, known as 'falsies'. Indeed, they were so necessary for the creation of the fashionable silhouette that the Corset Guild of Great Britain noted that three out of every four women were wearing falsies in 1955.[19] Falsies were hard inserts worn inside the bra, or stitched into the cups as seen here, and were almost the only way to achieve the exaggerated pointed breast shape that reached its height in the late 1950s, particularly around 1957. Another way to achieve it was with circular or whirlpool stitching around the cup, however this often required further padding at the point to reinforce the shape.

Long-line bra
Illa Knina
Britain (London), late 1950s
Nylon, foam rubber covered in knitted nylon, and nylon velveteen
V&A: T.852–1994

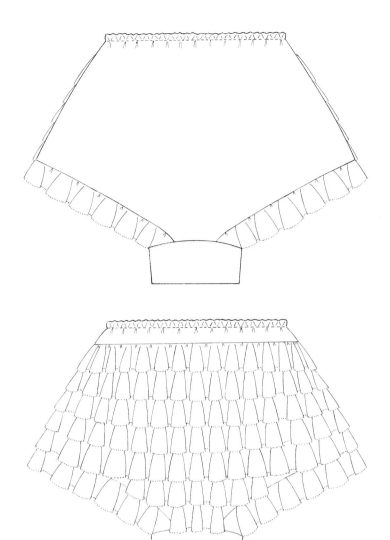

These knickers are completely covered at the front with tiers of nylon lace. The tiers add volume around the hips, creating a voluptuous and rounded shape. When worn under tulle petticoats they add further fullness to the skirt.

The hourglass figure was fashionable through the 1950s and early 1960s, and was shaped by a range of foundation garments designed to cinch the waist and emphasize the hips and bust. This type of figure was idealized in fashion magazines and on the couture catwalk, but reached its zenith in Hollywood, where pneumatic movie stars were introduced along with their symmetrical 'vital statistics'. In the 1950s, a sizing system called the 'hip spring' was popular, and was printed on garment and price labels to denote the ratio between the waist and hips.[20] For example, a 25-inch waist and 35-inch hip was a hip spring of 10 (10 inches). The desire for pronounced, hourglass hips caused some women to pad their hips with foam or rubber, or to pin ruched fabric to their underwear beneath their petticoats. Vere French, the wife of fashion photographer John French, noted that tiered or ruched knickers were particularly popular with slim girls.[21]

These knickers are made from nylon, which was developed before the war but only introduced commercially once the conflict was over. It revolutionized the underwear industry with its easy care qualities, and could be made into a vast range of fabrics, from crêpe and taffeta to Chantilly-style lace, as seen here. The affordability of nylon put apparently luxurious lingerie like this within reach of the average woman, and it became incredibly popular during the 1950s. The label in these knickers proudly states: 'Weavamill nylon for perfect fit'.

Knickers
Weavamill
Britain, late 1950s
Nylon and nylon lace
Bequeathed by Ruth Sheradski
V&A: T.295–1977

This full-length petticoat was worn underneath a lace evening gown, designed by the couture house of Jacques Fath. The gown was made for Cynthia Jebb (Lady Gladwyn), the wife of the British Ambassador to France, and worn at a reception for Queen Elizabeth II's visit to Paris in April 1957. It was given to her for free because the couture house knew it would bring them great publicity. The dress is historical in style, echoing the crinoline skirts of the 1860s.

The petticoat is designed, constructed and hand-finished with the same care and workmanship as the outer dress. It is made of silk taffeta, with a corseted strapless bodice and layers of tulle at the back to support the voluminous skirt of the evening dress. A length of stiff nylon net is ruched under the topmost layer of tulle to create a supporting bustle, adding a further kick to the train. The colours of the petticoat complement the evening gown, creating a base underneath the lilac lace. Both the petticoat and dress are fastened with hooks and eyes at the back, and assistance was required to put it on. For the state banquet, Fath sent Lady Gladwyn's vendeuse (her personal saleswoman and fitter) and an assistant to the embassy to dress and style her.[22]

Fath died in 1954, but the business was maintained by his widow, Geneviève. It was one of the most successful couture houses of the 1950s, and was known for figure-hugging and often rather risqué designs. Fath relied heavily on foundationwear to create the body shape he wanted, using either separate petticoats such as this one, or integral foundations sewn into the interior of his dresses. He also used traditional corsetry techniques for outerwear: he used whalebone to structure his tailored day suits, and used corset lacing as a glamorous feature of eveningwear.

Petticoat
Jacques Fath
France (Paris), spring/summer 1957
Silk taffeta and tulle, with nylon netting, spiral steel bones and metal hook-and-eye fastening
Given by Lady Gladwyn
V&A: T.173A–1974

INSIDE OUT

The way bedroom secrets have moved on to the street must be the fashion phenomenon of our times.

Vogue, 1991[1]

Outer garments have long reflected underwear motifs and techniques, but since the early 1980s fashion designers have comprehensively appropriated the aesthetics of underwear to make provocative and sexually charged statements about the body, sexuality and power.

This chapter includes two pieces by Vivienne Westwood, one of the primary figures of the 1970s punk movement. The punks subverted established rules about gendered dress, often wearing underwear and bondage gear as outerwear, and Westwood was one of the first designers to bring this avant-garde style to mainstream fashion. One of her early post-punk creations is a bra she and Malcolm McLaren designed to be worn over external layers. Included here, it is from the 1982–3 'Nostalgia of Mud' collection and is inspired by 1950s bra construction. Westwood also creates bodices directly inspired by eighteenth-century stays, and skirts inspired by bustles and crinolines, often using the collection at the V&A for research.

Visible underwear is not an entirely recent phenomenon, however, and some of the objects illustrated in this chapter show the historical precedent of visible or referenced undergarments. Seventeenth-century artists like Sir Peter

Lely (1618–80) painted aristocratic women in fashionable undress, with their chemises exposed and draped provocatively around their limbs, and the turn of the nineteenth century saw women wearing light 'chemise' dresses to emulate classical drapery. The March 1803 edition of *The Lady's Monthly Museum* magazine wrote about 'young ladies who were dressed or rather undressed in all nakedness of the mode'. A century later, Edwardian fashions also emulated underwear styles. Outer garments were decorated with techniques and trimmings previously associated with lingerie, such as lace inserts, baby-ribbon, and picot edging. Tea gowns, which began the century as loose but luxurious negligee-style house-coats worn only in the company of family or intimate friends, became semi-formal daywear by the 1920s, while the prevailing 1930s fashion for bias-cut dresses so emulated lingerie's palette and styling as to make under and outerwear all but indistinguishable from one another.

For centuries, the rules of decorum and display have shifted subtly and carefully around the subject of underwear. Today, vestigial underwear motifs or underwear worn overtly as outerwear is a common sight, and its visual language is an established part of fashion's lexicon.

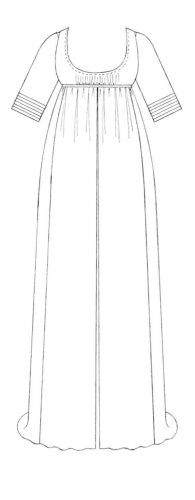
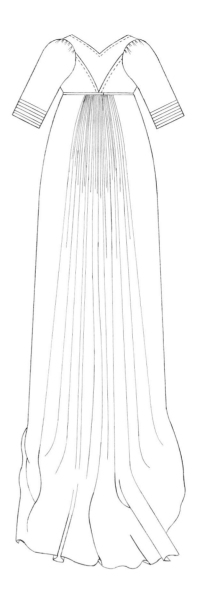

At the end of the seventeenth century there was a complete and dramatic change in fashion. Hoops, whalebone stays and rich embroidery were abandoned in favour of simple lines and plain fabrics – the most valued of which was fine muslin. Marie Antoinette first introduced the style to court in the 1780s, in her pursuit of a romantic, pastoral ideal; she even gave bolts of muslin as gifts to courtiers and friends.[2] However, the fashion became truly established following the French Revolution, as an emulation of the classical gowns of the ancient Greek republic.

In contrast to the voluminous style of previous decades, dresses were tubular, and skirts fell from just under the bust. They were often made from plain white fabrics, and so resembled traditional underwear that many considered them immodest. In 1800, *The Lady's Magazine* featured a 'Dialogue between a Lady and a Man-Milliner'. The Lady begins: 'Citizen, I am just come to town, pray have the goodness to inform me how I must appear to be in the fashion?' The milliner responds by suggesting that she removes her bonnet, petticoat, handkerchief, corset, and sleeves, leaving her in nothing but her chemise. He states finally: 'Tis an easy matter you see – to be dressed in the fashion you have only to undress!'[3]

Cartoonists and satirists intimated that women wore no underwear beneath the chemise dress[4], though British women still generally wore chemises, petticoats and modified stays (pp.82-4); some women wore 'invisible' tube petticoats of clinging stockinet to reduce bulk still further.[5] However, even with these foundations the body was perceptible. The writer Louis-Sébastien Mercier (1740–1814) wrote that some Parisiennes wore 'flesh-coloured knit-work silk stays, which stuck close to the body [and] did not leave the beholder to divine, but to perceive, every secret charm' of the body.[6]

This dress is made from diaphanous muslin imported from India, and is embroidered with floral patterns across its surface.

Dress
Britain, *c.*1800
Muslin embroidered in cotton thread
Given by Messrs Harrods Ltd
V&A: T.785&A–1913

Tea gowns cross the divide between underwear and outerwear. They were introduced in the 1870s, and were a mix of informal house-coat and luxurious negligee. They were usually loose-fitting and allowed women to loosen or remove their corsets and bustles while at home. They became increasingly popular at the beginning of the twentieth century, and were made from silks and satins with profusions of lace and ribbon. They were worn as dressing gowns around the home, but were also worn to entertain visiting female friends. The tea gown was the perfect vehicle for the Edwardian predilection for sensual and attractive dress, as espoused by couturiers such as Callot Soeurs and Lucile, who gave her tea gowns names like 'The Sighing Sound of Lips Unsatisfied'.[7] Tea gowns helped soften the distinction between private and public dress, and women became accustomed to being seen uncorseted. By the 1920s, versions of the tea gown were worn outside the house as semi-formal dress for garden parties and afternoon tea.

This tea gown was made by the Parisian couture house of Callot Soeurs, established in 1895 by the four Callot sisters: Marie, Marthe, Regina and Joséphine. They had all been taught lace-making by their mother, and initially specialized in blouses and lingerie, hand-worked with antique lace and ribbons. When they expanded into other forms of dress, their designs borrowed much from the aesthetics and techniques of lingerie. The house was successful and grew to become one of the most popular of the 1920s, training the important 1930s couturiere, Madeleine Vionnet (p.196).

This tea gown is made of pink silk damask with a leaf and flower pattern. It hangs loose and open at the centre-front, while the back features a sack back pleat from the shoulder to the hips, where it merges with the skirt. The skirt is slightly fitted into the waist at the hips. The sleeves are elbow length with a deep turned-back cuff. The edges of the gown are trimmed with a deep frill of tamboured net and ruched narrow-gauged ribbon and rosettes.

Tea gown
Callot Soeurs
France (Paris), 1905
Silk damask with tamboured net and silk ribbon; with silk lining
V&A: T.148–1967

During the late 1920s, the couturiere Madeleine Vionnet introduced the bias cut that dominated 1930s fashion. The technique, seen here, uses fabric cut diagonally to the grain, which means that it clings to the body and skims its contours. Typical of Vionnet too is the minimal seaming, the impeccable darting that shapes the integral turn-down collar, and the absence of any interfacing to interfere with the fall of the dress. Her skill in cut and construction caused *Time* magazine of 13 August 1928 to report that: 'Dressmakers concede to Madeleine Vionnet's mastery of the art of fitting . . . [Her] perfect lines . . . are the despair of copyists and imitators.'

Vionnet was influential in the adoption of lingerie aesthetics for fashionable dress; for example, the drawn thread work that creates the symmetrical pattern on this dress was traditionally more typically seen on underwear. Indeed, during the 1930s, underwear and outerwear shared similar, if not identical, construction and design. Both nightdresses and evening dresses were

cut on the bias, often in pastel and pale coral-coloured silk satins, crêpes and georgettes, with simple darts for extra shaping and very little trimming. Both featured cape sleeves and were fashionably worn with bolero jackets or short capes. In appearance, petticoats and nightwear were almost interchangeable with outerwear, and homogeneity of design ran through the layers of dress.

For the first time the natural waist and body was revealed. This was not the corseted torso of the nineteenth century, nor the flattened garçon style of the 1920s. Vionnet did not use integral corsetry or padding; she relied upon the natural form and movement of the body for shape, referencing classical drapery and the physicality of dancers like Isadora Duncan. The figure-hugging silhouette required a sleek foundation, which was ideally a toned, youthful body with defined but subtle feminine curves. Women that needed assistance to achieve the streamlined figure relied on girdles and bras, but they were required to be as smooth and imperceptible as possible beneath the fluid crêpes and satins.

Dress
Madeleine Vionnet (1876–1975)
France (Paris), mid-1930s
Bias-cut silk crêpe
V&A: T.196–1973

This dress directly echoes the lingerie of the late 1950s. In 1956, Carroll Baker starred as the eponymous protagonist of Tennessee Williams' film *Baby Doll*, appearing in a short but voluminous nightdress that popularized the style and gave it its name. The film was successful and critically acclaimed, but also highly controversial, attracting media attention for its overtly sexual content[8], and its inference would not have been lost on either designer or client. The baby doll nightdress was often made from sheer fabrics, revealing the body underneath. It developed from the use of new, semi-transparent nylons for nightdresses in the late 1940s and 1950s, from the shape of loose dressing gowns and bed jackets that flared outwards from the shoulders, and from the short A-line dresses traditionally worn by girls and, indeed, baby dolls. The baby doll nightdress was popular throughout the 1960s.

This black lace cocktail dress was designed by couturier Cristóbal Balenciaga for his autumn/winter 1958 collection. Balenciaga was known as a master of cut and construction, a perfectionist who used fabric to form sculptural and often abstract planes around the body. Various themes are evident in Balenciaga's work. He was deeply influenced by the traditional and religious dress of his native Spain, and his designs often feature visual echoes of the toreador, the flamenco dancer, and Basque folk dress, with black lace a particular favourite material. Another enduring theme in his work was the exploration of geometric shapes; throughout his careers he played with barrel, spherical and conical shapes.

The dress shown here abstracts the body while revealing the natural contours underneath. It is made of black lace with stiffened tiers that hang in a cone around the body. The lace overlays a fitted crêpe de chine sheath underdress, joined together only at the shoulders. When the dress is worn, the arms of the wearer press down on the lace, forcing the tiers to flare out, creating a fluid and responsive garment that moves with the body.

Baby doll dress
Cristóbal Balenciaga (1895–1972)
France (Paris), autumn/winter 1958
Crêpe de chine underdress, with lace overdress and satin bows
V&A: T.334–1997

The social and cultural upheavals of the 1960s rendered the underwear and lingerie of the previous decades and centuries obsolete in many ways. For hundreds of years the fashionable body had been shaped and padded by foundation wear, and moralists and social commentators had debated every subtle movement of hem or neckline. In the nineteenth century, the corset was worn with a corset cover in order to minimize the risk that even underwear might be visible, let alone the body itself, but the youth revolution of the 1960s broke with the traditions of previous generations, including the conventions of underwear and body covering.

This top is part of a range of transparent clothing designed by the couturier André Courrèges in 1968. The range is made of fine stretch chiffon, and was designed to be worn without underwear. Here the breasts are partially covered by squares of opaque cotton, however on other garments in the collection the torso is entirely transparent save for an ironic thick-knit polo-neck. In these and other designs, Courrèges played with the idea of the concealed and revealed body, and subverted expectations. He was the first designer to show a miniskirt on the Paris catwalk, revealing the legs to an unprecedented degree, and he presented collections with cut-away sections and clear plastic windows at the midriff, cleavage or buttocks.[9]

Courrèges launched his couture house in 1961, having worked for ten years as a pattern cutter for the master couturier Balenciaga (p.198), from whom he learned cutting techniques and a mastery of fabrics that allowed him to create bold geometrical shapes. He designed for athletic young women liberated from girdles, suspenders and prim tailoring: 'Women needed to be able to walk and run again. Our intention was to dress the youth, and for women to feel young in Courrèges.'[10]

Top
André Courrèges (b. 1923)
France (Paris), 1968
Stretch chiffon
Given by Baroness Helen Bachofen Von Echt
V&A: T.160–1983

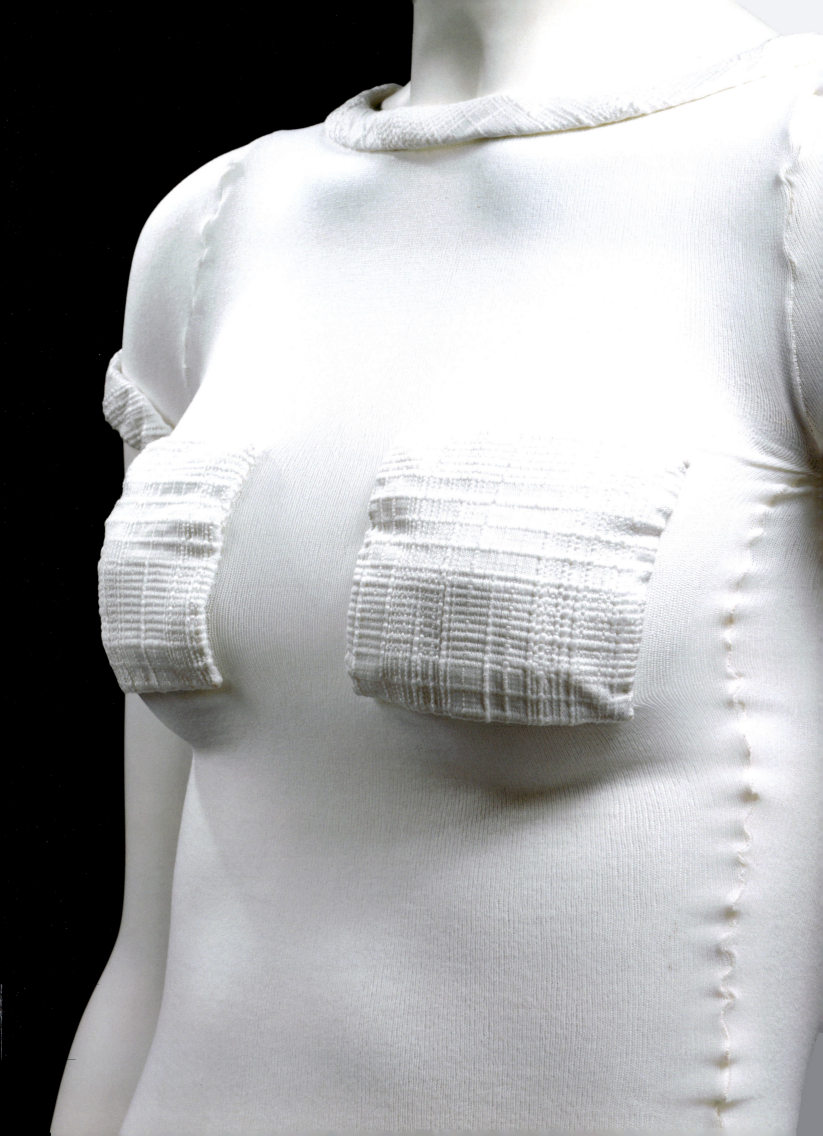

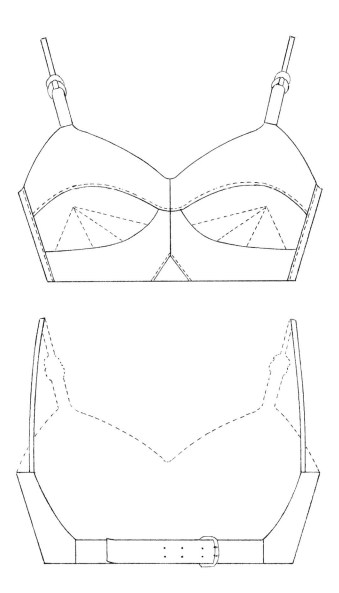

In 1971, Malcolm McLaren and Vivienne Westwood opened a shop on the King's Road in London, which became the informal headquarters of the punk movement. Initially it was named Let It Rock, but it was later variously called Too Fast To Live Too Young To Die, Sex, and Seditionaries. In 1980 it was renamed a final time as World's End, under which label this bra was made. During the early 1980s, McLaren became increasingly involved with music, and Westwood increasingly with fashion. They presented several successful catwalk shows, starting with the 'Pirates' collection of 1981, but parted ways in 1983.

This bra is from McLaren and Westwood's third collection, 'Buffalo' – also known as 'Nostalgia of Mud' – of autumn/winter 1982–3. The bra was part of several ensembles in the collection, and was designed to be worn on top of the outfit. McLaren and Westwood teamed ethnic influences and an earthy colour scheme with fine art and contemporary cultural references. The bra was worn over multi-layered ensembles inspired by indigenous Peruvian dress, and with cotton jersey dresses printed with Henri Matisse lithographs. The construction of the bra is historical, echoing the conical shape and undercup seaming of 1950s bras, however, the leather detailing and the rich brown colour subvert the 1950s aesthetic. Westwood encouraged people to try her designs out for themselves, saying: 'Take your mother's old brassiere and wear it undisguised over your school jumper and have a muddy face.'[11]

Bra
Malcolm McLaren (1946-2010) and Vivienne Westwood (b. 1941)
Britain, autumn/winter 1982
Synthetic satin lined with cotton, with leather strap and detail
Given by Mr Patrick Moore
V&A: T.238–1985

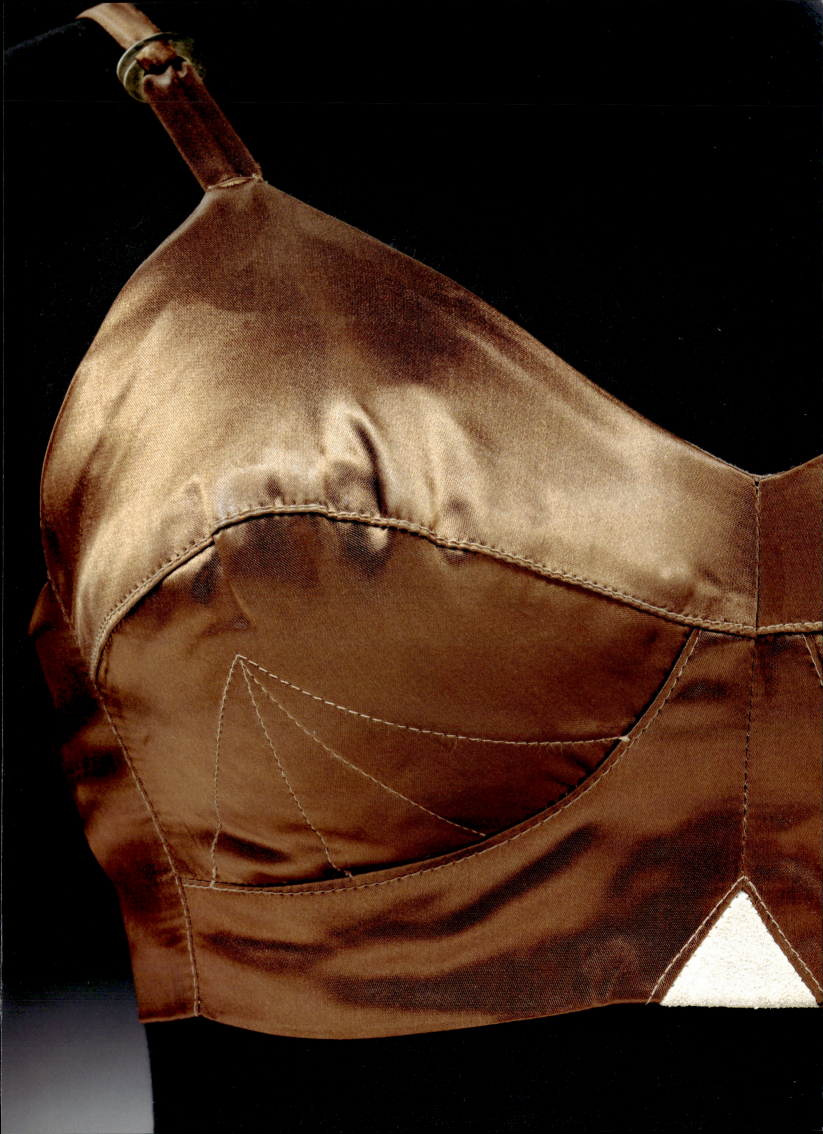

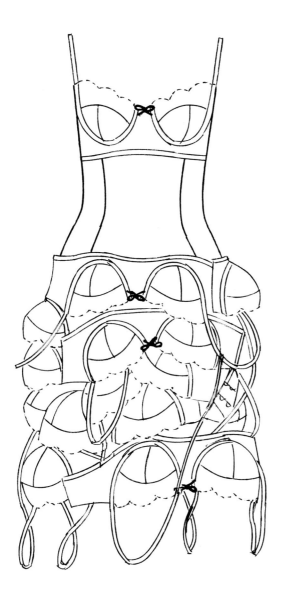 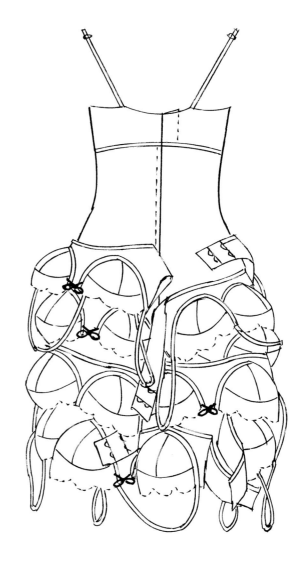

Franco Moschino was a designer who satirized the excesses of the fashion industry. Here he parodies the 1980s trend for using underwear as outerwear, and pushes it to an extreme. This dress is made from a Lycra power-net sheath, onto which a bra is attached at the bosom, and a further twenty at the skirt. The silhouette of the dress is that of a conventional cocktail dress, with a fitted bodice and a bell-shaped skirt. However, the shape is achieved by stitching the bras onto the garment upside down and leaving their straps to hang loose, reinterpreting a typical cocktail theme of tiered flounces and ribbons. Though he was a skilful pattern cutter and technically very capable, Moschino was a concept-driven designer and, as with this dress, he often took existing materials or designs and customized them to create new statement pieces.

Moschino trained as an artist at the Accademia delle Belle Arti in Milan, but funded his studies by creating illustrations for fashion magazines and soon developed a taste for design. He worked as an illustrator for Gianni Versace from 1971–7, and then briefly for the Italian house of Cadette, before setting up on his own in 1983. He retained the conceptual flair of art school, and his collections were innovative and often highly unusual.[12]

Though provocative, Moschino's designs were accessible and desirable and became highly sought after. He was embraced – perhaps unwillingly or accidentally – by the system he satirized. However, he continued to rebel against it with humour and self-awareness.

Evening dress
Franco Moschino (1950–94)
Italy (Milan), 1988
Lycra, machine-sewn cotton and polyester
Given by the designer
V&A: T.243–1989

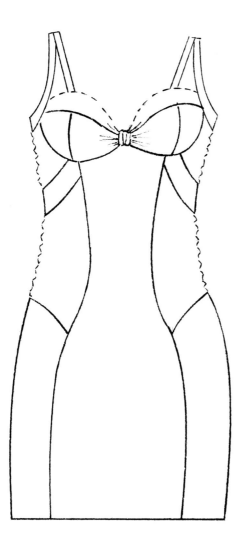
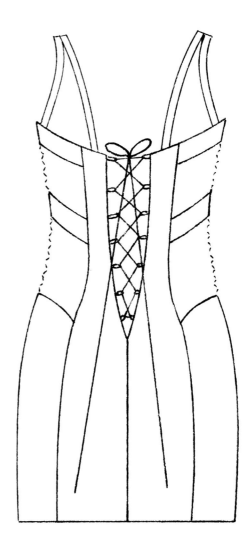

This is an example of the clinging micro-minidress that was fashionable in the 1980s and early 1990s. It is constructed from panels of Lycra, strategically positioned around the body and intersected with see-through net lace. The dress reveals the shape of the body and the skin underneath, and makes it clear that no underwear is worn. The back of the dress fastens with corset-style lacing, but here the body has become its own corset. Lycra dresses such as this epitomized the body-conscious culture of the 1980s and early 1990s, when fashionable women shaped their bodies with aerobics and diet regimes instead of whalebone. The net sections are made up of an irregular pattern with gathers and tucks, giving the impression of deconstructed weave, challenging the integrity of the dress as a complete or useful body covering.

Lycra was a fundamental part of the development of the toned, body-conscious ideal. Lycra and other makes of elastane (spandex) were an important component of the leotards and leggings of the 1970s fitness and dance craze, which spilt over into club and street wear in the early 1980s. In 1982 Azzedine Alaïa (born 1935) launched his fashion house with collections of skimpy Lycra dresses – for which he became known as the 'King of Cling' – and ensured that little black Lycra dresses became a high-fashion staple.

This dress was designed by the French born Val Piriou, who was named Innovative Designer of the Year in October 1990. It was part of her spring 1991 collection, which featured clinging and textured fabrics, decorative fastenings, and large scale weaves and knits that revealed the body. *The New York Times* of 16 October 1990, reported: 'The new name to drop was Val Piriou . . . She made her fashion-show debut to the live music of a New Orleans jazz band. Her clothes had so many openings they often looked more like underwear.'

Dress
Val Piriou (1963–95)
Britain (London), spring/summer 1991
Lycra and ruched elastic with net lace inserts
Donated by Marie Paule Piriou in memory of her daughter
V&A:T.225–1998

This dress was part of Gianni Versace's spring/summer 1994 haute couture collection, presented in Paris. In this collection, as in many others, Versace created glamorous outerwear that was overtly inspired by lingerie. This very short minidress is made of crushed silk with an embroidered lace yoke and a section of smocking across the midriff that falls into sunray pleats. There is a slight A-line kick at the hem that adds fullness and fluidity of movement to the skirt.

The collection was dominated by underwear-inspired designs. One of the two major strands of the show was a series of chemise slips, of which this dress was a part. They were presented in various colours, including vibrant yellow, purple and various shades of green, in addition to black and white. They were shown with matching stockings and heels, and their hems reached just below the buttocks, to occasionally reveal lace knickers and stocking tops. The other strand was a series of black dresses that featured cuts, slashes, and oversized safety-pins reminiscent of bondage gear. One of these dresses was famously worn by Elizabeth Hurley to the premiere of the 1994 film, *Four Weddings and a Funeral*.

Dress
Gianni Versace (1946–97)
Italy (Milan), spring/summer 1994
Crushed silk with lace and embroidered inserts
V&A: T.215–2004

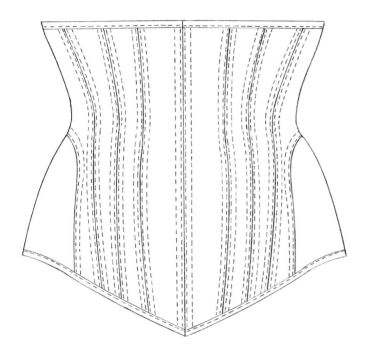 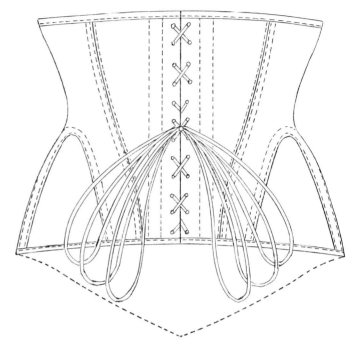

As a result of the introduction of elastane fabrics and a fitness craze that valued a toned and exercised body, sales of foundationwear dropped dramatically during the 1970s. DuPont conducted a survey to understand the trend, and found that 54 per cent of young women rejected corsetry and girdles because they were associated with old age, or old-fashioned value systems and chauvinism.[13] As a result, Du Pont and other underwear manufacturers rebranded their foundationwear to appeal to the new market, producing streamlined, dance-inspired bodysuits. The corset, as a universal staple of women's wardrobes, was now an historical memory for young women. However, in the early 1980s, fashion designers such as Vivienne Westwood and Jean-Paul Gaultier reappropriated the corset as provocative outerwear, and wearing a corset as an outer garment was touted as a statement of powerful femininity. Corsets were teamed with evening or cocktail dresses, or worn as bustier-style tops under tailored jackets.

This corset is made of black nylon satin, with contrasting red floral embroidery on the front and back panels. Twelve hooks and eyes at the centre-front provide a flat, streamlined abdomen. As opposed to the traditional steel busk and slot-and-stud fastening, hooks and eyes allow the modern wearer to bend and sit, and are a feature of corsets worn as outerwear. Flexible plastic bones at the side accentuate the curve of the hip and emphasize the waist.

It was designed by Rigby & Peller, the traditional corsetry company established in the 1930s, and corsetiers to the Queen since the 1960s (p.154). In 1982 the company was bought by June Kenton, but the Royal Warrant did not necessarily transfer to her, and Kenton was called to the palace to be personally approved by the Queen. Kenton retained the Royal Warrant, confirming the company's reputation for traditional corsetry. However, she also expanded the business to include online sales, ready-to-wear, swimwear and outerwear ranges.

Underbust corset
Rigby & Peller
Britain (London), 1996
Nylon satin, with machine-embroidered net, back lacing and hook-and-eye fastening
V&A: T.469–1996

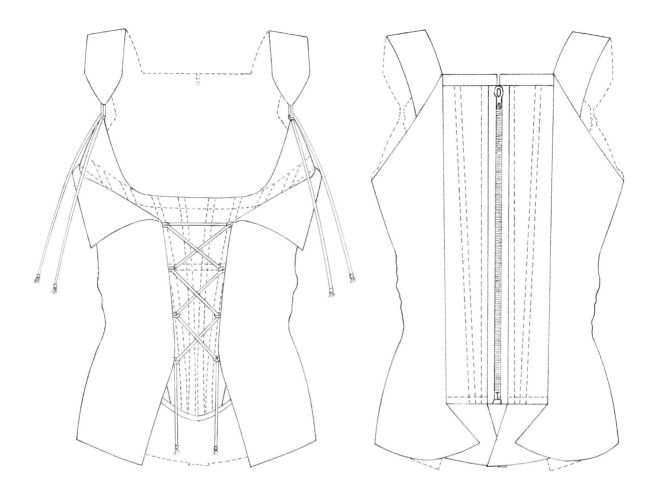

Since she presented her first catwalk show in 1981, Vivienne Westwood has been increasingly recognized as among the world's foremost fashion designers. One of the most enduring influences on her work is historical dress, and many of her collections have drawn on the styles, silhouettes, materials and techniques of the past. In particular, the use of historically inspired corsetry has become one of her signature themes. In her autumn/winter 1987–8 'Harris Tweed' collection, Westwood presented the Statue of Liberty corset. Designed as a glittering boned evening bodice that compressed the breasts and pushed them upwards, it was hugely influential in promoting the use of corsetry as mainstream fashion, along with the work of designers such as Jean-Paul Gaultier. In 1990, Westwood presented her 'Portrait' collection, with corset bodices that emulated eighteenth-century stays and featured images of paintings by François Boucher (1703–70).

Her corsets not only echo the shape and look of historical stays, their construction is also closely modelled on the originals. Westwood has studied the collection at the V&A, including the pattern and structure of seventeenth- and eighteenth-century clothing. However, Westwood reinterprets these designs for a contemporary market, using plastic boning, power-nets and zips to create lightweight, comfortable versions of the style. Other underwear items that have influenced Westwood are the bustle and the cage crinoline, which she reinterpreted for her 1985 'Mini Crini' collection.

This corset is inspired by eighteenth-century stays. It features front lacing, lace-tied shoulder straps, and a stomacher with horizontal, diagonal and vertical bones that create a rounded décolletage and conical torso shape similar to the stays of the 1770s (p.78). It is made of a white cotton piqué, seamed at the back to two panels of Lycra, with plastic bones at either side of a centre-back zip fastening. The cotton piqué wraps around the body to lace at the centre-front over the stomacher. The stomacher is triangular in shape, and the cotton piqué disguises the fact that it is stitched to a Lycra power-net that circles the body all the way around to the two centre-back panels.

Corset
Vivienne Westwood (b. 1941)
Britain, 1996
White cotton piqué, plastic boning and Lycra, with zip
Given by Jane Levi
V&A: T.14–2002

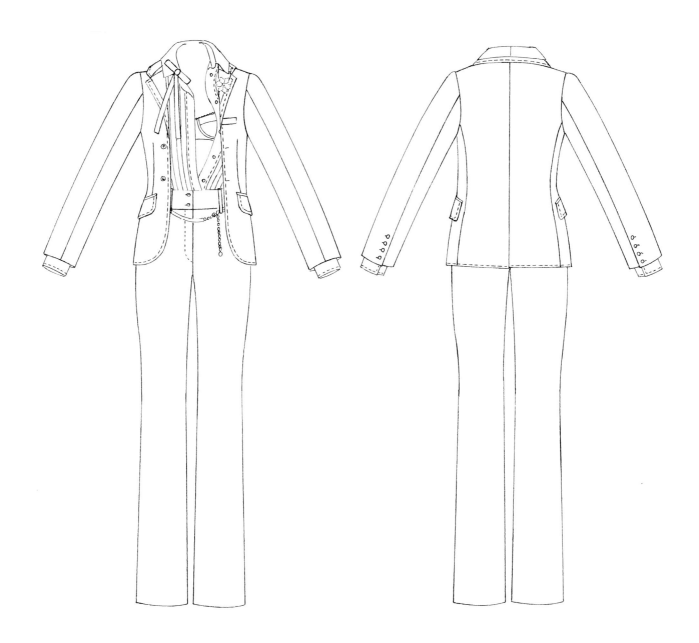

Domenico Dolce (born 1958) and Stefano Gabbana (born 1962) opened their first boutique in 1987, becoming famous for sleek Italian tailoring, and for corsetry and underwear designed as outerwear, or, as *Harper's Bazaar* magazine said in 1996, 'sexy alla Italiana boudoir-for the boardroom fashion'.[14]

This velvet tuxedo suit for women was part of the Dolce & Gabbana ready-to-wear collection of autumn/winter 2004–5, presented in Milan. The collection played with conventions of gendered dress, presenting sharp tailoring alongside transparent chiffons, lace and visible underwear. The drainpipe trousers and fitted jacket are made of silk velvet with silk satin lapels. The shirt is shown open to reveal the bra, and the bow tie is askew, so while it is not as revealing as many other ensembles, it hints towards undress and uses the visible underwear to subvert conventions by both

feminizing and sexualizing the traditionally male look. The rest of the collection presented tailored jackets worn without shirts, short and lacy chemise dresses worn under fur jackets, and transparent black dresses accented with bright underwear.

This suit was inspired by Yves Saint Laurent's (1936–2008) 'Le Smoking' collection of 1966, which first introduced androgynous tuxedos for women as high fashion. The look was popularized by fashion photographer Helmut Newton (1920–2004) for French *Vogue* of September 1975. Newton's photograph shows a woman in a masculine tuxedo with sleeked-down hair, smoking in a dark Parisian alley. An unpublished photo from the same series shows the suited model alongside a naked woman. It is this ambiguity of power roles and sexuality that Dolce & Gabbana aimed to reinterpret for the catwalk.

Ensemble
Dolce & Gabbana
Italy (Milan), autumn/winter 2004–5
Velvet trouser suit, cotton shirt with pleating, silk bow tie, and gold and paste Swarovski belt clip and brooch
V&A: T.2:1-6–2005

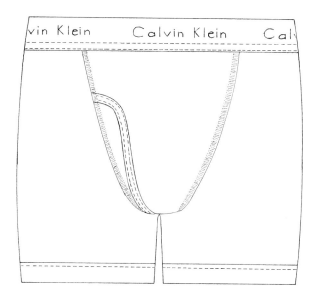
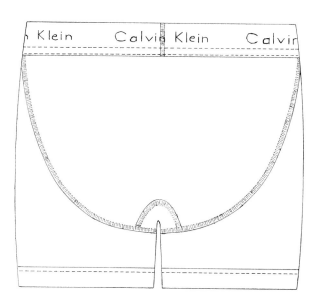

The history of underpants for men has largely been one of functionality. For the majority of the twentieth century, male underpants were based upon the three basic designs of long johns, Y-fronts and boxer shorts. They were largely plain and white, and were certainly not revealed in public. In 1982, Calvin Klein launched a range of branded cotton jockey briefs, marketed with a billboard and magazine campaign featuring athlete Tom Hintanhaus standing in nothing but white briefs. This was the first time that male underwear had been marketed as a desirable fashion item, and also the first time that the sexualized male body was presented in this way to a mainstream, mass audience. The media furore that greeted the campaign ensured its success, and for many, 'Calvins' became a synonym for underpants.

In the early 1990s, young men began styling their clothes so that their underpants were visible over the top of their low-slung jeans, and as part of hip-hop culture it has become a prevalent global trend. Klein capitalized on this, and in 1992 ran prominent billboard and television advertisements featuring rap star and actor Mark Wahlberg in low-slung Calvin Klein jeans revealing the visible branded waistband of his underpants. Kate Moss appeared alongside Wahlberg, similarly styled in low-rise jeans and no top, in-keeping with Klein's unisex ethos and products. Klein's range of underwear for women was launched in 1983, and was modelled on men's boxer shorts, complete with fly. Klein proclaimed that gender specific underwear was an old-fashioned concept: 'Lingerie is a term of the past. It's just underwear.'[15]

Underpants
Calvin Klein (b. 1942)
USA, 2005
Cotton with elasticized waistband
V&A: T.8–2005

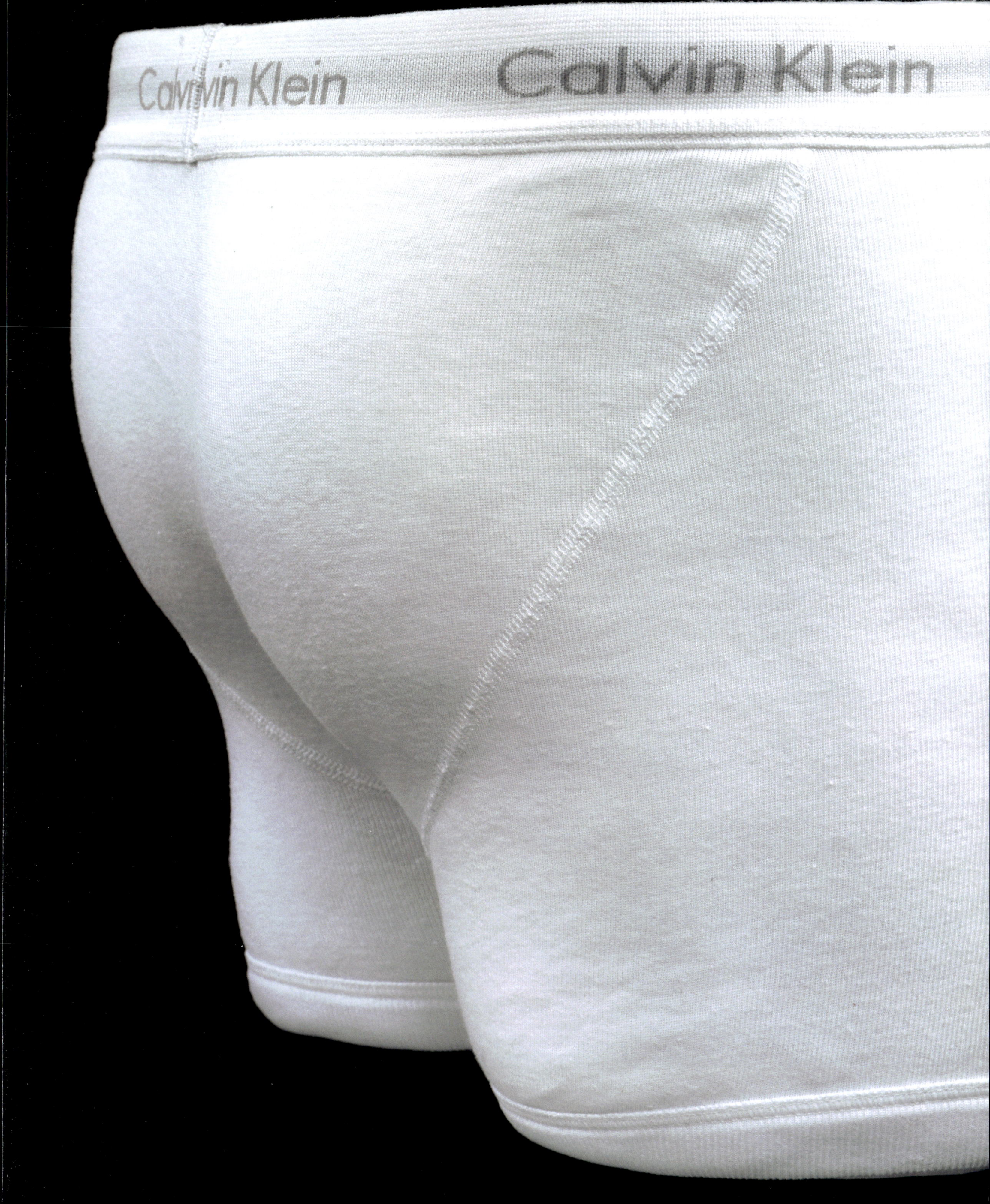
Calvin Klein
Calvin Klein

NOTES

INTRODUCTION

1   Dior (2007), p.73.

COVERING UP

1   Lady Colin Campbell, *Etiquette of Good Society* (London, 1893), p.77.
2   Raverat (1960), p.260.
3   Dr Daumas cited in Steele (1996), p.216.
4   Cunnington (1992), p.137.
5   Drawers were still regarded by some as semi-scandalous. The best selling author and doctor Edward Tilt warned that if women wore drawers or trousers they might assume masculine manners. See Tilt (1852), p.193.
6   Ribeiro (1986), p.63.
7   Anon., *The English Theophrastus or The Manners of the Age* (London, 1706), pp.53–5.
8   *Tatler*, 28 March 1710.
9   Anne Fremantle (ed.), *The Wynne Diaries*, III (London, 1935), p.324.
10 Cunnington (1992), p.172.
11 Jane H. Adeane (ed.), *The Early Married Life of Maria Josepha, Lady Stanley* (London, 1899), p.404.
12 Robert Ellis, *Official Descriptive and Illustrated Catalogue: The Great Exhibition* (London, 1851), p.485.
13 Cunnington (2004), p.126.
14 Cunnington (1992), p.217.
15 Carter (1992), p.159; see also selected advertisements in *The Times*, 2 January 1897, 12 July 1904, 11 October 1904.
16 Warren (2001), p.38.
17 Ibid., p.75.
18 Carter (1992), p.94.

DECORATION

1   Dior (2007), p.73.
2   Lucile (Duff-Gordon) cited in Ewing (1978), p.107.
3   Pritchard (1902), pp.20–1.
4   Elisabeth Geddes and Moyra McNeill, *Blackwork Embroidery* (New York, 1976), p.46.
5   Arnold (1988), pp.149–151.
6   Robert Campbell, *The London Tradesman* (London, 1747), p.215.
7   Ewing (1978), p.33. See also Farrell (1992).
8   See Farrell (1992), p.41, 57 & 64.
9   Cunnington (1992), pp.153–4.
10 Alice de Laincell, *L'Art de la toilette chez la femme* (Paris, 1885), p.37.
11 Mrs G.E. Dixon to the V&A, April 1928. V&A Archive, registered papers, RF 1928/4394.
12 Cunnington (1992), p.218.
13 Duff-Gordon (1932), p.66.
14 Comtesse de Tramar, *Le Bréviaire de la Femme* (Paris, 1903).
15 Pritchard (1902), p.20.
16 Lucile Archives, V&A: Archive of Art and Design.
17 *The New York Times*, 26 October 1911; *The Times*, 12 February 1964.
18 Shteir (2004), pp.148–9.
19 *L'Officiel de la Mode*, nos. 46–158, 1925–34.
20 Fogarty (1960), p.44.
21 *Biggleswade Today* (*The Biggleswade Chronicle*), 16 September 2008. One of Kayser Bondor's factories was based in Biggleswade, Bedfordshire, from 1938–91.
22 Fogarty (1960), p.43.
23 Haye (1996), p.181.
24 David Giles, *Media Psychology* (London, 2002), p.106.

CONTROL AND CONSTRICT

1   *La Vie Parisienne, année* 5, 1868, p.744.
2   Ewing (1978), p.22; also Robert Crowley ('Her mydle braced in . . . at the paste wyfes hand') cited in Waugh (1954), p.27.
3   See Kenneth R. Andrews, *Trade, Plunder, and Settlement: Maritime Enterprise and the Genesis of the British Empire, 1480–1630* (Cambridge, 1984), p.341; Farley Mowat, *A Whale for the Killing* (Mechanicsburg, PA, 2005), p.6.
4   Arnold (1988), p.146.
5   Thomas Johnson (trans.), *The Work of That Famous Chirurgian Ambroise Parey* (London, 1649), pp.581–2.
6   Harold Koda, *Extreme Beauty: The Body Transformed* (New York, 2001), p.75
7   François-Alexandre-Pierre de Garsault, *L'Art du Tailleur* (Paris, 1769).
8   Steele (2001), p.29.
9   Lucy Johnston, *Nineteenth-Century Fashion in Detail* (London, 2005), p.170.
10 Wimbledon tennis star Elizabeth Ryan (1892–1979), cited in Teddy Tinling, *Sixty Years in Tennis* (London, 1983), p.24.
11 V&A Archive: registered papers, RF 84/985.
12 Waugh (1954), pp.88 & 111.
13 Gustav Jaeger, *Selections from Essays on Health Culture and the Sanitary Woollen System* (London, 1884).
14 Cited in Summers (2001), p.28.
15 Eric Jay Dolin, *Leviathan: The History of Whaling in America* (New York, 2007), p.356.
16 Warren (2001), p.30.
17 Ewing (1978), pp.109–10; and Steele (2001), p.84.
18 Duff-Gordon (1932), p.76.
19 See Newman, Bressler and Proctor (1997), p.59; and Buckley and Fawcett (2002), p.63.
20 Buckley and Fawcett (2002), p.11.
21 Twilfit advertisement in *The Times*, 11 November 1924.
22 Thomas Hancock, *Personal Narrative of the Origin and Progress of the Caoutchouc or India-Rubber Manufacture in England* (London, 1857), p.101.
23 See Ewing (1978), pp.143–6.
24 Haye (1996), p.187.
25 Warren (2001), p.62.
26 Silhouette Ltd: marketing records, 1957–c.1989. V&A Archive of Art and Design: AAD/1994/21.
27 Daniel Delis Hill, *As Seen in Vogue: A Century of American Fashion in Advertising* (Texas, 2007), p.93.
28 *Vogue* (UK), March 1965, p.32.
29 All quotes from 'Joe Corré and Serena Rees: Sex and the City', *The Independent*, Monday 29 July, 2002.
30 *The Independent*, 24 November 2001.

FASTENINGS

1   Eliza Farrar, *The Young Lady's Friend* (New York, 1857), p.179.
2   Though the illustrations show the standard, if not predominant, lacing techniques of their age, various lacing styles appear throughout the book due to the idiosyncratic nature of individual lacing preferences.
3   Vita Sackville-West, *The Edwardians* (London, 1983), pp.39–40.
4   Cunnington (1992), p.106.
5   Measurements include the front busk panel, which measures 19cm at its widest point along the top.
6   Newman, Bressler and Proctor (1997), p.87.
7   Fontanel (2001), p.49.
8   Ewing (1978), p.58.
9   Ewing (1978), p.96.
10 Dr Gustav Jaeger, *Essays on Health Culture* (London, 1887), p.167.
11 Steele (2001), pp.75–6; and Steele (1985), p.165.
12 Cited in Summers (2001), p.60.
13 Roxey Anne Caplin, *Health and Beauty* (London, 1864), p.xii.
14 *Hansard*, 21 March 1944, vol. 398.
15 Marjorie Janko (Miss Marene), *The Production of Modern Lingerie* (Unpublished: 1951). V&A Archive of Art and Design: AAD/1998/14/70.
16 Farrell (1992), p.79.
17 *UK Lingerie and Underwear Retailing Report 2009* (London, 2009), pp.6–7.

SUPPORT AND UPLIFT

1   Farrell-Beck and Gau (2002), pp.ix–xv.
2   US Patent US24033, 17 May 1859 (European Patent Office).
3   US Patent US494397, 11 January 1893 (European Patent Office).
4   Volumizing bust bodices from around this time, whose only function was to add mass and not lend support, are found in the next chapter.
5   Ewing (1978), p.115.
6   Paul Poiret, *My First 50 Years* (London, 1931), pp. 72–3.
7   See: 'Engineers famous for their wobble help build £2m bra', *The Telegraph*, 26 October 2000.
8   Farrell-Beck and Gau (2002).
9   Cunnington (1992), p.115; and Steele (2001), p.30.
10 *Spirella Corset Accessories* (Meadville, PA, 1913), pp.3 & 24.
11 *The Times*, 7 May 1914.
12 Several US patents for Kestos are registered under the names Rosamond L. Kennedy and Rosamond Klin; see Farrell-Beck and Gau (2002), pp.78 & 208. She is elsewhere identified as Rosalind Klin; see Ewing (1978).
13 *L'Officiel de la Mode*, no. 127, March 1932, p.78; no. 129, May 1932, p.49; nos. 319–20, Winter 1948, p.38.
14 *L'Officiel de la Mode*, no. 137, January 1933, p.9.
15 US Patent 1798274, 31 March 1931 (European Patent Office).
16 US Patent 1970920, 21 August 1934; and US Patent 2104725, 11 January 1938.
17 'Gernreich the Outrageous', *The Washington Post*, 28 April 1985.
18 Akiko Busch, *Design for Sports: the Cult of Performance* (New York, 1998).
19 Haye (1996), p.186.
20 Rachel Worth, *Fashion for the People: A History of Clothing at Marks & Spencer* (Oxford, 2006).
21 See 'Playtex, Gossard gird themselves for battle of bras', *Advertising Age*, 11 October 1993; also 'Bra wars; The bra business and technology', *The Economist*, 2 December 2000; and Leighton Linslade Virtual Museum (www.leighton-museum.org.uk), June 2008.

VOLUME

1   Henry Fielding, *The Works of Henry Fielding* (London, 1849), p.697.
2   Cunnington (1992), p.197.
3   *The Female Spectator* (1744–6), cited in Cunnington (1992), p.70.
4   Waugh (1954), p.61.
5   A fine unbleached linen, so-named because it was originally imported from Holland.
6   Besançon was a centre of the watch-making industry, where spring steels would have been readily available for experimentation and invention.
7   No. 1729, 22 July 1856 (British Library).
8   Hippolyte Taine, *Notes on England* (London, 1872), pp.68–9.
9   *Punch*, vol. XLVIII, July 1865; *London Society*, vol. X, 1866, pp.234 & 273; *The Times*, 4 August 1864; Ewing (1978), p.74.
10 Waugh (1954), p.166.
11 *The Englishwoman's Domestic Magazine*, October 1862, vol. V., p 286.
12 For a small selection see *The Times*, 19 November 1859; 15 August 1862; 25 November 1862; 23 March 1863; 29 November 1866; 3 July 1867.
13 Carter (1992), p.159.
14 Rothstein (1999), p.143 (cat entry 77).
15 Steele (1985), p.221; see also Ella Adelia Fletcher, *The Woman Beautiful* (New York, 1900), p.437.
16 *Spirella Corset Accessories* (Meadville, PA, 1913), pp.3 & 9.
17 Warren (2001), p.90.
18 *Vogue* (UK), February 1953.
19 Ewing (1978), p.162
20 Page (1981), p.54.
21 John French Archive. V&A Archive of Art and Design: AAD F.342/6.
22 Miles Jebb (ed.), *The Diaries of Cynthia Gladwyn* (London, 1995), pp.208–12.

INSIDE OUT

1   *Vogue* (UK), October 1991, p.167.
2   Antonia Fraser, *Marie Antoinette* (New York, 2001), p.163.
3   *The Lady's Magazine* (1800), cited in Waugh (1954), p.129.
4   Ribeiro (1986), p.120.
5   Francis Paget Hett (ed.), *The Memoirs of Susan Sibbald 1783–1812* (London, 1926), p.138.
6   Cited in Ribeiro (1986), p.125.
7   Lucile Archives, V&A: Archive of Art and Design.
8   *Time*, 24 December 1956.
9   Giles Lipovetsky, *The Empire of Fashion: Dressing Modern Democracy* (Princeton, 2002), p.91.
10 Mme Coqueline Courrèges quoted in 'In the beginning, there was Courrèges', *The Independent*, 8 November 2001.
11 Claire Wilcox, 'Vivienne Westwood: 34 years in fashion', Essay for National Gallery of Australia, 2 November 2004–30 January 2005.
12 'Franco Moschino', *The New York Times*, 20 September 1994; 'Obituary: Franco Moschino', *The Independent*, 21 September 1994.
13 Ewing (1978), pp.172–3.
14 Cited in Newman, Bressler and Proctor (1997), p.92.
15 'Calvin's New Gender Benders', *Time*, 5 September 1983.

GLOSSARY

Baleen (Fr. *Baleine*): See *whalebone*.

Bandeau: A *brassiere*-style garment designed to flatten the bust; fashionable in the 1920s.

Basque: A lightly-boned *corset*, covering the breasts and waist but not the hips; often incorporating suspenders.

Batiste: A fine, plain-weave fabric, usually made from cotton or linen.

Bloomers: Ankle-length trousers for women, worn underneath calf-length skirts; advocated by American dress reformer Amelia Bloomer in the early 1850s. *Drawers* are sometimes called 'bloomers' because of their visual similarity.

Bodies: A sixteenth-century term for a boned bodice. Also known as 'whalebone bodies', 'a pair of bodies', 'bodys', or (Fr.) *'corps à la baleine'*. Referred to in the plural because they were often made in two parts. See also *stays*.

Bodysuit: A one-piece streamlining garment made of *elastane* fabric, covering the torso and often fastening with press studs at the crotch. Introduced in the 1960s and popularized during the fitness craze of the 1970s.

Bones: Narrow strips of hard material used to stiffen and shape bodices and *corsets*. The term derives from *whalebone*, the historically preferred boning material. Other boning materials include reeds, quills, compressed paper, flat or *spiral steel*, and plastic.

Bra: A diminutive term for the *brassiere*, the word 'bra' entered common parlance in the 1930s.

Brassiere: A garment worn around the chest to shape and support the breasts. Previously known as a *bust bodice*, the term 'brassiere' was used in American *Vogue* in 1907. It is probably an appropriation of the Old French for harness or shoulder strap. The French name for a brassiere is *'soutien gorge'* (breast support).

Buckram: Thick linen or cotton, stiffened with glue or paste.

Busk: A piece of rigid material, such as wood or *whalebone*, inserted into a *casing* at the centre-front of *stays* or *corsets* to reinforce a straight and upright torso. See also *split busk*.

Bust bodice: A short bodice to shape and support the breasts, worn over the chemise. It was introduced in the mid- to late nineteenth century in response to a fashion for low-cut corsets. A precursor to the *brassiere*.

Bust improver: A structured or ruffled *bust bodice* worn to augment the bosom. It was worn over the *chemise* and *corset* towards the end of the nineteenth century and beginning of the twentieth century.

Bustier: A long-line *brassiere*, extending to the top of the waist.

Bustle: Padding worn underneath the back of the skirt at the lower back or buttocks, either as an integral part of a *crinoline* or *crinolette* petticoat, as a separate pad filled with horsehair, straw or down, or as a wire frame tied around the waist.

Cambric: A fine, plain-weave cotton or linen, used to line corsets.

Cami-knickers, or Teddy: One-piece lingerie garment incorporating *camisole* top and wide-leg knickers, often made of satin.

Camisole: A sleeveless lingerie top; it developed from the *corset cover* of the nineteenth century.

Casings: The narrow pockets along the length of *stays* or *corsets* created by rows of stitching, into which the *bones* are placed. Also the channel through which a drawstring is threaded.

Chemise: A simply cut, knee- or calf-length underdress, predominantly made of linen until the nineteenth century when cotton was used more widely; more rarely made from hemp, wool or silk. It was the base layer to all other layers of underwear. Previously known as a *shift*, it was called a chemise from the late eighteenth century onwards.

Combinations: *Drawers* and *chemise* combined into one garment, and introduced in the 1870s. Summer or evening combinations were made of light fabrics such as silk; winter versions were made of flannel and wool.

Cording: An alternative method of *corset* shaping that was cheaper and more flexible than *whalebone*; made of twisted reed or plant fibres.

Corselette (also corselet): A one-piece control garment incorporating *brassiere* and *girdle*, with shoulder straps and integral suspenders.

Corset cover: A bodice worn over the *corset*, later known as a *camisole*. It appeared around 1840, and was worn to hide the top of the corset from accidental view and to provide a smoothing layer between the *corset* and dress.

Corset: A waist- and torso-shaping garment stiffened with boning and tightened with laces, typically encasing the bust and hips for an hourglass figure. Previously known as *stays*, the term corset was popularly used from the early nineteenth century.

Coutille (also coutil): A tightly-woven herringbone *twill* fabric, usually made of cotton. Traditionally used for corsetry as it is durable and resists stretching.

Crinoline: From the French word *'crin'*, for horsehair. A nineteenth-century bell-shaped petticoat stiffened with a variety of materials, including horsehair, cane or *whalebone*. A frame petticoat made from spring steel wire hoops, known as a cage crinoline, was introduced in the mid-1850s.

Crinolette: A small *crinoline*, flat at the front but full at the back. Popular from the mid-1860s, when the bell-shaped crinoline fell out of fashion.

Directoire knickers: Loose knickers worn at the beginning of the twentieth century, gathered at the waist and knee. Named for the style of drawers worn in France during the 'Directoire' period of the late eighteenth century.

'Divorce' brassiere: A *brassiere* designed to separate the breasts.

Drawers: Long, voluminous underpants, worn in Britain from the early nineteenth century onwards. See also *pantaloons* and *combinations*.

Elastane: A generic term for the synthetic, high-tensile, *elastic* fabric introduced by DuPont USA in 1959. Also known as spandex (USA) and elastomerics (Europe, prior to the mid-1970s). See also *Lycra*.

Elastic: A stretch material capable of resuming its original shape, usually rubber elastic. Rubber elastic was developed for use in clothing by the British Rubber Company from the 1820s onwards, but was little used in underwear until the development of viable methods for transporting liquid rubber in the late 1920s. Prior to this, 'elastic' referred to stretchy, knitted fabrics like stockinet. See also *lastex*.

Farthingale: The 'Spanish farthingale' was first recorded towards the end of the fifteenth century and worn in Britain and France until the middle of the sixteenth century. It was a cone-shaped petticoat created with hoops of cane or *whalebone* stitched into stiffened fabric. The later 'French farthingale' radiated outwards from the waist to create a drum shape, supported by spokes. It was fashionable from the middle of the sixteenth century into the seventeenth century. A similar effect was achieved by tying a padded roll around the waist.

Flossing: Fan-shaped surface stitching at the top and bottom of *whalebone casings*, to reinforce the *bones* and secure them in place. It also doubled as decorative detailing.

Girdle: A control garment extending from the waist, down over the hips to the upper thighs, usually with integral *suspenders*. Made with elasticized panels and sometimes reinforced with boning. See also *roll-on* and *wrap-around*.

Holland: Fine, plain-weave linen, historically imported from Holland.

Jumps: An eighteenth-century laced bodice worn instead of stays, often made from stiffened or strong fabric, but with little or no boning. Worn informally at home or during pregnancy, and by working women for mobility.

Lastex: A yarn with a rubber *elastic* core, wound around with cotton, rayon, nylon or silk thread. It can be woven or knitted and provides a durable two-way stretch much used in *girdles* and *corselettes*. It was introduced by the Dunlop Rubber Company in 1929 and was widely used until the introduction of *elastane* fabrics in 1959.

Lawn: Fine, plain-weave linen or cotton with a silky finish, historically made in Laon, France.

Lingerie: Derived from the French *'linge'* (linen), and refers to *shifts, chemises, shirts, drawers*, and nightshirts. These items were historically the only clothes regularly laundered. Today understood to mean seductive or revealing women's underwear, usually made of lace, chiffon or satin materials.

Lycra: A brand name *elastane* registered by DuPont (USA) in 1959.

Nainsook: A fine, light-weight *muslin*.

Negligee: A luxurious and decorative dressing gown.

Nylon: A versatile, easy-care, synthetic fibre patented by DuPont in 1937; it can be knitted or woven, and blended with other fibres.

Marquisette: A sheer, gauze-like material; it can be made from cotton, silk, or synthetic fabrics.

Muslin: A fine, plain-weave, undyed cotton.

Pantaloons: Tight male leg coverings, usually knitted; worn as outergarments towards the end of the eighteenth century. Also a late eighteenth-century and early nineteenth-century term for women's underpants; they were longer and more closely fitted than later *drawers*, and were variously known as 'trowsers' or 'pantalettes'.

Panty-girdle: A control garment with legs, covering waist to mid-thigh. Widely advertised in the 1960s as it could be worn with youthful fashions like jeans.

Power-net: Tensile *elastic* netting. Used in panels for control garments such as *corselettes* and *girdles* from the mid-twentieth century in the form of elasticized *nylon* netting, and particularly from the 1960s onwards following the introduction of *elastane*.

Princess petticoat: One-piece skirt and bodice petticoat without a waist seam. Popularly worn at the end of the nineteenth century and beginning of the twentieth century to fit under streamlined fashions.

Rational dress: A clothing style advocated by late nineteenth-century dress and health reformers who were opposed to tight corsetry and heavy petticoats.

Rayon: A synthetic fibre patented in 1892 and popularly used in clothing manufacture from the 1920s onwards. Because of its sheen, it was sometimes called Artificial or Art Silk.

Roll-on: A *girdle* made entirely of elasticized material with no fastening; it is pulled or rolled on over the hips.

S-bend: A style of *corset* popular in the 1900s, particularly around 1905. It was cut low underneath the bosom and extended down over the hips. It was made with a straight *busk* that pressed into the groin, causing the pelvis to tilt backwards, the back to arch, and the chest to thrust forwards.

Shift: The seventeenth- and eighteenth-century term for a *chemise*; previously known as a smock.

Shirt: Until the mid-twentieth century, a man's undergarment. A sleeved, thigh-length, T-shaped garment, predominantly made of linen until the nineteenth century, when cotton was used more widely; more rarely made from hemp, silk or wool. It was the base layer for other undergarments until the introduction of undervests in the mid-nineteenth century.

Side hoop: Eighteenth-century oval-shaped petticoat frame, made from hoops of cane or *whalebone* covered in fabric. It protruded outwards horizontally to the hip, and at its most exaggerated it created a square- or fan-shaped skirt as seen from the front.

Slip: A light petticoat with bodice and skirt.

Slot-and-stud: Metal hook-and-eye fastening system, fixed to the steel *split busks* of *corsets*. Patented in 1848 and still used on *corsets* to the present day.

Spiral steels: *Corset bones* made of thin steel wires curled into flat spiral strips. Introduced in the early twentieth century, largely replacing *whalebones*.

Split busk: Two metal strips that run the vertical length of the *corset* and fasten together at the centre-front, reinforcing its shape and allowing the wearer to fasten and remove it on her own. Patented in 1829, but not commonly used until the introduction of the *slot-and-stud* fastening in 1848.

Spoon busk: A metal *split busk* that curves at the lower half to cup the abdomen, ostensibly introduced to relieve pressure on the internal organs. Popular in the 1870s and 1880s.

Stays: The seventeenth- and eighteenth-century term for a boned underbodice. Stays created a rigid conical torso, and featured tabs around the bottom that flared over the hips. Also known as 'a pair of stays' as they were often made in two parts. Later known as a *corset*. See also *bodies*.

Suspenders: Clasps to hold up stockings, worn on a belt or as an integral part of *corsets, girdles, corselettes,* or *basques*. Introduced to Britain in the 1870s. Rendered largely obsolete by the introduction of *tights*.

Swiss belt: A type of lightly boned *corset*, cut low under the bust and high over the hips.

Tightlacing: The practice of lacing the *corset* by increments to create an extremely small waist circumference.

Tights (USA Pantyhose): Stretchable one-piece leg coverings, extending up to the waist. Introduced in the 1960s, largely replacing stockings and *suspenders*.

Twill: A type of weave creating rows of parallel diagonal ribs. See also *coutille*.

Waspie (Fr. *Guêpière*): An elasticized belt reinforced with boning, designed to cinch the waist and give a pronounced hourglass, or 'wasp-waist', figure; fashionable in the late 1940s and 1950s.

Whalebone: Keratinous plates around the upper jaw of baleen whales, used to sift food. Once extracted, it can be cut along the grain into narrow strips, and is both strong and pliable. Whalebone moulds slightly to the shape of the wearer when warmed by her body heat. Baleen whales were hunted to near extinction for oil and whalebone in the nineteenth century.

Wrap-around: A *girdle* wrapped around the body, partly overlapping, and fastened with hooks and eyes or a zip down one side.

FURTHER READING

Arnold, Janet, *Patterns of Fashion 4: The cut and construction of linen shirts, smocks, neckwear, headwear and accessories for men and women c. 1540–1660* (London, 2008)

Arnold, Janet, *Queen Elizabeth's Wardrobe Unlock'd* (Leeds, 1988)

Buckley, Cheryl, and Fawcett, Hilary, *Fashioning the Feminine: Representation and Women's Fashion from the Fin de Siècle to the Present* (London & New York, 2002)

Carter, Alison, *Underwear: The Fashion History* (London, 1992)

Cox, Caroline, *Lingerie: A Lexicon of Style* (London, 2000)

Cunnington, C. Willett and Phillis, *The History of Underclothes* (London, 1992)

Cunnington, C. Willett, *Fashion and Women's Attitudes in the Nineteenth Century* (New York, 2004)

Dior, Christian, *The Little Dictionary of Fashion* (New York, 2007)

Doyle, Robert, *Waisted Efforts: An illustrated guide to corset making* (Nova Scotia, 1997)

Duff-Gordon, Lucy, *Discretions and Indiscretions* (London, 1932)

Ewing, Elizabeth, *Dress and Undress: A History of Women's Underwear* (London, 1978)

Farrell, Jeremy, *Socks & Stockings* (London, 1992)

Farrell-Beck, Jane, and Gau, Colleen, *Uplift: The Bra in America* (Philadelphia, 2002)

Fogarty, Anne, *The Art of Being a Well Dressed Wife: with provocative notes for the patient husband who pays the bills* (Suffolk, 1960)

Fontanel, Beatrice, *Support and Seduction: A History of Corsets and Bras* (New York, 2001)

Hawthorne, Rosemary, *Bras: A Private View* (London, 1992)

Haye, Amy de la (ed.), *The Cutting Edge* (London, 1996)

Kunzle, David, *Fashion and Fetishism: Corsets, Tight-lacing and Other Forms of Body Sculpture* (London, 2004)

Kyoto Costume Institute/Fashion Institute of Technology, *Undercover Story* (Kyoto, 1983)

Martin, Richard, and Koda, Harold, *Waist Not: The Migration of the Waist 1800–1960* (New York, 1994)

Newman, K., Bressler, K., and Proctor, G., *A Century of Lingerie* (New Jersey, 1997)

Page, Christopher, *Foundations of Fashion: The Symington Collection* (Leicester, 1981)

Pedersen, Stephanie, *Bra: A Thousand Years of Style, Support and Seduction* (Newton Abbot, 2004)

Pritchard, Eric (Mrs), *The Cult of Chiffon* (London, 1902)

Probert, Christina, *Lingerie in Vogue* (London, 1981)

Raverat, Gwen, *Period Piece: A Victorian Childhood* (London, 1960)

Reynolds, Helen, *A Fashionable History of Underwear* (Portsmouth, 2003)

Ribeiro, Aileen, *Dress and Morality* (London, 1986)

Rothstein, Natalie (ed.), *Four Hundred Years of Fashion* (London, 1992)

Saint-Laurent, Cecil, *A History of Ladies Underwear* (London, 1968)

Salen, Jill, *Corsets: Historical Patterns & Techniques* (London, 2008)

Shteir, Rachel, *Striptease: The Untold History of the Girlie Show* (Oxford, 2004)

Steele, Valerie, *Fashion and Eroticism: Ideals of Feminine Beauty from the Victorian Era to the Jazz Age* (Oxford, 1985)

Steele, Valerie, *Fetish: Fashion, Sex and Power* (New Haven & London, 1996)

Steele, Valerie, *Paris Fashion: A Cultural History* (Oxford, 1988)

Steele, Valerie, *The Corset: A Cultural History* (New Haven & London, 2001)

Summers, Leigh, *Bound to Please: A History of the Victorian Corset* (Oxford and New York, 2001)

Tilt, Edward, *Elements of Health and Principles of Female Hygiene* (London, 1852)

Warren, Philip, *Foundations of Fashion: the Symington Corsetry Collection 1860–1990* (Leicester, 2001)

Waugh, Norah, *Corsets and Crinolines* (London, 1954)

MUSEUM COLLECTIONS

The following museums hold national or major dress collections.
Please note that many local and regional museums also hold excellent examples of fashionable and domestic underwear.

Furniture, Textiles and Fashion Dept
Victoria and Albert Museum
South Kensington
London SW7 2RL
www.vam.ac.uk

Museum of London
London Wall
London EC2Y 5HN
www.museumoflondon.org.uk

Royal Ceremonial Dress Collection
Kensington Palace
London W8 4PX
www.hrp.org.uk

Fashion Museum
Bennet Street
Bath BA1 2QH
www.museumofcostume.co.uk

Gallery of Costume
Manchester City Galleries
Platt Hall
Manchester M14 5LL
www.manchestergalleries.org

Symington Collection of Corsetry,
Foundation & Swimwear
Harborough Museum (Leicestershire
County Council Heritage Services)
Adam & Eve Street
Market Harborough LE16 7AG
www.museums.leics.gov.uk

Brighton Museum & Art Gallery
Royal Pavilion Gardens
Brighton
East Sussex BN1 1UE
www.brighton.virtualmuseum.info

National Museums of Scotland
Chambers Street
Edinburgh EH1 1JF
www.nms.ac.uk

Musée de la Mode et du Textile
Les Arts Décoratifs
107 Rue de Rivoli
Paris
France
www.lesartsdecoratifs.fr

Musée Galliera
10 Avenue Pierre 1er de Serbie
Paris
France
www.paris.fr

Museo del Traje
Avenida Juan de Herrera
Madrid
Spain
www.museodeltraje.mcu.es

The Costume Institute
The Metropolitan Museum of Art
Fifth Avenue
New York City
New York
USA
www.metmuseum.org

Fashion Institute of Technology
Seventh Avenue at 27 Street
New York City
New York
USA
www.fitnyc.edu

Kent State University Museum
Kent State University
Kent
Ohio
USA
www.kent.edu/museum

Philadelphia Museum of Art
Benjamin Franklin Parkway
Philadelphia, PA
USA
www.philamuseum.org

Museum of Fine Arts
Avenue of the Arts
465 Huntington Avenue
Boston, Massachusetts
USA
www.mfa.org

Texas Fashion Collection
University of North Texas
School of Visual Arts
Denton
Texas
USA
www.tfc.unt.edu

Phoenix Art Museum
Central Avenue & McDowell Road
Phoenix
Arizona
USA
www.phxart.org

Los Angeles County Museum of Art
5905 Wilshire Blvd
Los Angeles
CA 90036
USA
www.lacma.org

Royal Ontario Museum
100 Queen's Park
Toronto, Ontario
Canada
www.rom.on.ca

**Museo Nacional de la Historia
del Traje**
Chile 832
Ciudad Autónoma de Buenos Aires
República Argentina
www.funmuseodeltraje.com.ar

Kyoto Costume Institute
103 Shichi-jo
Goshonouchi Minamimachi
Kyoto
Japan
www.kci.or.jp

Powerhouse Museum
500 Harris Street
Sydney
Australia
www.powerhousemuseum.com